Mohawk Recon

Mohawk Recon

*Vietnam from Treetop Level
with the 1st Cavalry, 1968–1969*

RUSSELL PETTIS

McFarland & Company, Inc., Publishers
Jefferson, North Carolina

LIBRARY OF CONGRESS CATALOGUING-IN-PUBLICATION DATA

Names: Pettis, Russell, 1946– author.
Title: Mohawk recon : Vietnam from treetop
level with the 1st Cavalry, 1968–1969 / Russell Pettis.
Other titles: Vietnam from treetop level with the 1st Cavalry, 1968–1969
Description: Jefferson, North Carolina : McFarland & Company, Inc., Publishers, 2021 |
Includes index.
Identifiers: LCCN 2021038627 |
ISBN 9781476687360 (paperback : acid free paper) ∞
ISBN 9781476645254 (ebook)
Subjects: LCSH: Pettis, Russell, 1946– | United States.
Army. Cavalry Division, 1st. | Vietnam War, 1961–1975—
Personal narratives, American. | Vietnam War, 1961–1975—
Aerial operations, American. | Mohawk (Reconnaissance aircraft) |
Soldiers—United States—Biography. |
BISAC: HISTORY / Military / Vietnam War
Classification: LCC DS558.4 .P483 2021 | DDC 959.704/34 [B]—dc23
LC record available at https://lccn.loc.gov/2021038627

BRITISH LIBRARY CATALOGUING DATA ARE AVAILABLE

ISBN (print) 978-1-4766-8736-0
ISBN (ebook) 978-1-4766-4525-4

On the cover: OV-1C Mohawk in Vietnam
(artwork by Mark Karvon; www.markkarvon.com);
author relaxing while reading the *Stars and Stripes*

Printed in the United States of America

*McFarland & Company, Inc., Publishers
Box 611, Jefferson, North Carolina 28640
www.mcfarlandpub.com*

Table of Contents

Preface
Vietnam, May 1968–May 1969

Before there were drones, there were real live people who flew in relatively small, unarmed airplanes, taking aerial photos with a nose camera, a belly camera, a side-looking airborne radar system or an infrared target detection system that used heat differentiation to find targets on the ground in the dark. I was one of those. I was known as a technical observer, or TO for short. There were two of us in the cockpit: the pilot (usually a commissioned officer) and the observer (a highly trained enlisted man). The airplane we flew was a Grumman OV-1 Mohawk C model equipped with the cameras and the infrared system; it was a twin turboprop built for short takeoffs and landings on unimproved runways. The Mohawk was fast and maneuverable and could withstand quite a bit of punishment (i.e., damage caused by incoming bullets, unimproved runways and sometimes tree branches when we flew at the treetop level).

There were several Mohawk aviation companies throughout Vietnam: the 131st, 73rd, 244th and 225th aviation companies and two ASTA (aerial surveillance and target acquisition) platoons. One ASTA platoon was assigned to the 1st Infantry Division ("The Big Red One") in the Mekong Delta, and my ASTA platoon was part of the 1st Air Calvary Division. The Cavalry units covered all of I Corps bordering the DMZ (demilitarized zone) and extending to the Laos border. Our platoon consisted of six Mohawk aircraft, four pilots, ten or twelve TOs, six Mohawk crew chiefs, an imagery interpreter and various support troops, totaling a maximum of thirty people.

All of the people mentioned in this book are real, but their names have been changed (with the exception of my friend Phil and Alan the Aussie, who never mentioned his last name). In addition, all of the events described actually happened.

Come with me in the cockpit and around the compound as we fly

My new Nomex fire-retardant flight suit.

C model OV-1 Mohawk.

missions, live in tents, eat mostly C-rations, watch out for snakes (as well as mosquitos and other things that carry diseases), and do other interesting things, such as hit Marines with boomerangs, avoid Highway 1 Viet Cong (VC) ambushes, pull guard duty on the green line and many other things besides fly. For six months we covered the DMZ out to the border with Laos; during the last six months I served in-country, we covered the Cambodian border and surrounding areas in III Corps when the entire 1st Cavalry Division was moved south. We were assigned to fly out of Vung Tau and told to use the 73rd Aviation Company's mess hall for food but continued to live separately in our own area; however, this time we lived in wooden and screen-wall hooches with two-man rooms with walls and a door. We even had mama-sans who cleaned our rooms and washed our clothes for fifty cents a week. The rest of the Cavalry was spread out through III Corps and headquartered in Phuoc Vinh in the jungle somewhere near the Cambodian border. The flying to cover target missions in III Corps was very different from I Corps, as the terrain was very flat except for a 3,200-foot mountain called Nui Ba Den that you had to look out for in the dark.

Climb into the cockpit with me as I bring those missions to life.

Introduction

This book details many of my flying and non-flying experiences in Vietnam with the 1st Cavalry. Come fly with me as I describe my first combat assault mission in Vietnam, a daytime photo recon mission in the A Shau Valley. Look out the cockpit windows at the tracers converging on our Mohawk as we run up the valley at three hundred feet with the power and prop levers at maximum levels. Come with me as we fly at seventy-five feet over a riverside trail, taking photos with the belly camera. Feel the excitement as we buzz a fire support base located on a flat mountaintop and look directly into the faces of the artillery guys standing thirty feet below us. Listen to the radar technician informing us of the two bogeys (Migs) on our tail chasing us out of Cambodia. Look out the cockpit window just as five rounds from a 37 mm anti-aircraft gun lock onto us and fire a volley (those 37 mm rounds looked like flaming basketballs as they blasted by the nose of our aircraft, followed by five more next to my wing and another five as they passed just beneath our belly). Come on guard duty with me on the green line and spot movement in front of our bunker, visible through a starlight scope—the movement comes closer and becomes a tiger. Jump with me out of a burning airplane that caught fire on takeoff. Look into the darkness with me as we search for a UFO that the radar net has determined to be directly in front of us and watch for Cobra gunships that have been scrambled to assist us in the hunt for the UFO. Look out the side window and shudder as we fly directly through a B-52 strike, with the resulting explosions rocking the airplane and bouncing us all over the sky. Listen as I instruct a new first lieutenant about the dangers of low-level flying under a bridge and learn what happens to him soon after our get-to-know-the-territory flight. Sit with me and some Aussie grunts around a bonfire as a group of New Zealand Maori grunts perform a haka for us. These are just a few of the experiences I will share in this book.

The first six months were spent in I Corps in Phu Bai near the DMZ and the last six months with the Cavalry outside of Saigon, patrolling the Cambodian border. I was awarded the 1st through the 17th Air Medals for flying more than 300 missions. Sometimes, especially near the DMZ and the A Shau Valley and the terrain between, we would fly three or four missions per day, including infrared target detection at night, after which we would land, refuel and get airborne for a full day of visual recon and camera missions.

I have tried to remain apolitical with the exception of my criticism of the directive to disarm all Mohawks in Vietnam and the other situation of not being able to do anything about receiving anti-aircraft fire from Cambodia.

The living conditions were terrible for my first six months in-country, with the leaking tents, rats and lack of hot food. The food situation was caused by our lack of having our own mess hall and by the flight time we experienced every day and night. When the division moved south, our lifestyle improved dramatically with hooch life and better food. We continued to fly incredible hours, but not as demanding as in I Corps.

The Vietnam that I saw from the cockpit, versus on the ground, especially in I Corps was a beautiful country, full of wooded or jungled steep mountains with deep valleys filled with streams that eventually emptied into slow-moving rivers in broad valleys. These slow moving rivers provided water for the innumerable rice paddies and small villages. The rivers emptied into the ocean that contained dozens, if not hundreds, of off-shore islands. Each appeared to be a paradise with white sandy beaches, palm trees and other fruit bearing trees. Best of all, they were mostly uninhabited.

The Vietnam topography in III corps was strikingly different that I Corps where we had steep rugged mountains, but in III Corps, in the area around Saigon, the country was flat and transitioned to rice paddies towards the Mekong Delta. The rest of the area towards Cambodia and west was comprised of thick jungle with few if any roads or villages, just miles of jungle.

The land and seashore was strikingly beautiful in so many ways that I felt that under different circumstances, this land and seacoast would be a perfect tourist vacation destination. Some of the experiences are humorous, but many are not and describe life-or-death situations. Other stories deal with members of my aerial surveillance and target acquisition platoon and the things they chose to pursue as well as our daily routines. I do not voice any political views or opinions but focus on describing getting the mission accomplished.

I also describe my homecoming from Vietnam and my last year in the Army, fulfilling my obligation and returning to school with the assistance of the GI Bill to finish my BA as well as an MBA and an MA. This book fulfills a need to share many of my experiences about what some of us who were not grunts or helicopter pilots did during our year in Vietnam.

Vietnam is with me today like it was yesterday, and I am grateful that so many times, when things could have turned out badly, they didn't.

1

The Letter

You knew it would arrive, but you were not looking forward to receiving it. The letter appeared in late spring 1967 when my grandmother called me from the lobby counter of the small Massachusetts post office where I worked part time, attending college the rest of the time. I had the most governmental-sounding title of "temporary indefinite," which meant that I was an employee temporarily and indefinitely.

My grandparents lived in the same town as me but had a post office box and only picked up their mail once a month. My grandmother held out a letter addressed to me at my parents' street address that somehow had been sorted into her and my grandfather's post office box. I could tell from fifty feet away what the letter was and who it was from.

"Greetings." That was how all the draft notices began, followed by the instructions for you, the recipient, to follow. "You are hereby instructed to report at such and such a time at the Springfield, MA, Selective Service Center for your mandatory physical. If you have a medical condition that would prevent you from serving in the military, bring a letter from your family physician detailing your malady and the reason that condition would prevent you from serving in the military." The time came for the physical, and I passed with flying colors.

My friend from junior high and high school, Phil, received his letter at the same time I did. Phil was also working part time at the post office and going to school, and we discussed our courses of action; he had his physical at the same time as mine, and he passed too. We decided that rather than being drafted with a guarantee of Vietnam, we should visit some recruiters to see what was available if we enlisted. We immediately passed the Marine recruiter and said no to the Navy; the Coast Guard was full, as was the National Guard, which left the Air Force and the Army. The Air Force seemed like a possibility, but the enlistment period was longer, so we went to the Army recruiter and spent the afternoon taking test after test. With both of us in college, we were used to long, boring tests. The test results came back, and Phil had a strong interest in finance, while mine came back with results that led the recruiter to say to me, "Here is the MOS book of military occupations—take your pick." I took the book and was instantly overwhelmed by the endless choices. I finally said to the recruiter, "Which jobs aren't being used in Vietnam?" He asked me whether I liked to fly, and I said, "Don't know, as I have never been in an airplane." "Well, here is a brand new aviation job that isn't used in Vietnam—just Germany and Korea. It is called an airborne sensor specialist, where you fly around taking pictures and stuff."

He then told Phil and me about the "buddy plan" where you and a buddy enlist and are sent to basic training together. We signed on the dotted line and were told that we would be notified about when and where to report for transportation to our basic training location. My girlfriend, who soon after became my wife, was not pleased with my decision, but I said, "Germany, not Vietnam and not infantry; we will have a ball driving all over Europe."

Phil and I got our orders to report to Springfield, Massachusetts, for transport to Fort Dix, New Jersey, for basic training. On the appointed day, Phil and I boarded a bus bound for New Jersey; we sat together and talked about what we had gotten ourselves into. At Fort Dix, we got off the bus, and that was the last time we saw each other until three years later when we both returned to civilian life working at the post office again. During basic training, we were given tests, and evidently I did well on them, as I was offered OCS (Officer Candidate School) after basic training. I should have asked more questions or had better advice, but I was told that the only field open in OCS was infantry. I quickly decided that I did not want to go to Vietnam as an infantry officer. Had I received better guidance, I would have known that after receiving my commission I could apply for additional specialized training, such as flight school, intelligence, finance, and so on, but I was not advised of those options.

Phil went to Fort Polk, Louisiana, for AIT (advanced individual training) and stayed there for his entire tour of duty. I went from Fort Dix, New Jersey, to Fort Huachuca, Arizona, for my five months of training before going to, wait for it, Germany ... well, not quite, unless Bien Hoa is on the Rhine and the 1st Cavalry Division was guarding Denmark.

My wife and I got married at Fort Huachuca with the guys from my class in attendance. I was allowed to live off-post, and we found a nice trailer in downtown Sierra Vista, Arizona, just minutes from the main gate to Fort Huachuca. I needed transportation to get from Sierra Vista and onto the fort to make morning formation, so I looked around, and a mechanic at the local Dodge dealership had for sale just what I wanted. It was a 1958 DeSoto with the push-button automatic transmission. The car was grey and pink two-tone. The Dodge mechanic was a couple of years older than me and guaranteed the car. He told me that if anything went wrong, I should call him at home and he would repair the car. I took him at his word and found out soon after that he was a man to be trusted.

One Saturday my wife and I drove the DeSoto the seventy-five miles from Fort Huachuca into Tucson for the day. We were driving around in a nice neighborhood when a rainstorm hit and the car died. My wife was seven months pregnant at the time, and I told her to wait in the car while I went to a nearby house to ask to use their phone. I knocked on the door, and it was answered by a nice woman and her husband, along with their son and his girlfriend. They could tell that I was military and assumed that I was Air Force, as Davis-Monthan Air Force Base was close. I told them that I was stationed at Fort Huachuca and that my car had broken down and asked if I could use their phone to call my technician friend. I called and told him what had happened and the address of where I was. During the time I was talking on the phone, the homeowners had set a plate at the table for me to join them for dinner, I told them that I couldn't, as my wife was in the broken-down car. Before I could react, the husband rushed out the door with an umbrella and brought my wife in the house. These people would not be denied helping us by having us join them for dinner. Their son and his girlfriend, who were our age, invited us to go out with them, but my wife was tired, and we asked if they would mind taking us to the closest motel. They would have none of that and insisted that we spend the night with them and led us to their guest bedroom.

I awakened at about seven in the morning to the scent of freshly brewed coffee, bacon and eggs. Just then, the doorbell rang, and, to my surprise, my friend, the former owner of the DeSoto, stood there smiling. I said to him, "Let's go look at the car, and maybe you can tell what's wrong with it." He said, "I fixed it—the coil or alternator failed, and I replaced both of them. I had an extra key for the car that I had forgotten to give you. You are good to go." I stood there flabbergasted: it was early Sunday morning, and this guy had driven over seventy-five miles to get here, had diagnosed the problem, had the spare parts with him and had repaired the car, all done before 7:00 a.m. He said, "I told you that if anything went wrong with the car to let me know and I would take care of it." He was an extraordinary person and a man of his word. Along those same lines, the people who took us in, fed us and insisted we use their guest bedroom will forever live in my heart. When I returned from Vietnam and returned to Fort Huachuca to serve out the remainder of my enlistment, my wife and I took our baby daughter to introduce her to those people who had shown us so much concern and caring.

I found myself tasked with the unenviable task of waking my fellow classmates each morning as I arrived at the barracks. Typically, the guys in the top bunks would unscrew the light bulbs above their bunks, and when I went into the barracks and turned on the light switch, nothing happened. I would then turn on a radio, and each morning from radio station KOMA in Oklahoma City, the DJ would play the song "Get on Up" and dedicate it to the troops at Fort Huachuca, Arizona. I would crank up the volume, and finally the guys would come to life, and we would then go about our morning tasks of cleaning the latrine and shower area, sweeping the floor and using the buffer to ensure that any scuff marks were gone because quite often several guys would wrestle on the floor and leave scuff marks everywhere. We buffed those out, making the floor shiny, therefore avoiding extra duty. The guys made sure that their bunks were made Army style so that a quarter would bounce if one was dropped on the bunk covers and finally that our boots were shined before making it to our morning formation in the street outside our barracks.

We would stand in the street for inspection while the morning winds blew cold air from the Huachuca mountains that, in the winter, were snow covered for much of the time. After inspection, we were off to the mess hall for breakfast and then to the airfield for classes. We learned about the target systems in the Mohawk, along with the radios and, importantly, navigation and map reading. We were issued a hand-sized tool to aid in navigation and speed calculations called an E6B navigation tool. It had a rotary center with figures on it and around the outside edge, which was stationary, more numbers. You used this tool to calculate heading, distance and time to a target. For example, while flying, you needed to determine the flying time to the next target; you would turn the dial to the heading, then turn to aircraft speed and distance to the target, and you would look at the information and see that at the present heading and speed, you would be over your target in X number of minutes. If you carried a stopwatch, you would start it as soon as the airplane turned to its heading. If you didn't have a stopwatch, you simply looked at your watch and told the pilot and yourself that you would be over the target in so many minutes at such and such a time.

During our training at Fort Huachuca, there was a persistent rumor that after completing Airborne Sensor School, we would receive additional training and be appointed as warrant officers. Unfortunately, this story turned out to just that—a rumor.

Arizona was a great place and an incredible change for us New Englanders. There was the desert—mountains, cacti, wild horses—and then the climate. Fort Huachuca was located at 5,000 feet and offered a panoramic view of the bowl-shaped desert and mountains that were twenty-five miles away in every direction, with Mexico just over the mountains directly behind us. Having grown up watching westerns on TV and seeing cowboy and Indian movies, I was very excited to be in the Wild West. There were actual ghost towns not too far away that begged to be explored. We found one ghost town one day that was off the beaten track on a dirt trail. The town was located at the mouth of a box canyon and contained a main street with several still-intact buildings. There was a saloon, general store, small hotel, blacksmith shop, sheriff's office and several other buildings. All of the furniture was gone, as well as anything else considered valuable, but the saloon bar was still there, and it was in good condition. I assume that in the box canyon were old gold and silver mines, but I thought about the presence of rattlesnakes in the area and decided not to do any box canyon mine exploring. The excitement of finding this ghost town in decent condition and reliving history was incredible.

The town of Tombstone was not far from Fort Huachuca, and when we visited, it had not changed from the time of the OK Corral days. The town sheriff drove into town with a four-wheel-drive pickup, went behind the sheriff's office and came out into the street a few minutes later riding a horse. This was not for the tourists' benefit, as we were the only non-locals in town at the time; rather, this was how he patrolled the town and its immediate outskirts. There was also the Bisbee open-pit copper mine that looked to be five miles deep. The surrounding mountains contained old-time tales of their own, with the cavalry looking for the Apache chief Geronimo, who terrorized the area and even penetrated into Mexico. The mountains directly behind the fort led to Mexico and were crisscrossed with trails and a few very narrow roads that led directly into Mexico. These mountains and all the others surrounding the fort and the valley were pockmarked with abandoned gold and silver mines that had long ago been depleted. We heard of two guys from Fort Huachuca who were exploring a mine in the mountains behind the fort and found a model A Ford parked in the mine entrance, just out of sight. It had been there for years and was in good condition considering that it had been hidden in a mine for who knows how long. They pulled it out, replaced the tires, towed it back to the fort, tinkered with the engine, got it running and drove it around the fort. Who knows what else is hiding out of sight in those mines? Once we had a mountain lion run across the road in broad daylight in front of us when we were exploring the area.

The climate offered perfect flying weather, and the Mohawk pilots took advantage of the conditions to fly around the clock. My first flight in a Mohawk was impressive, as the pilot, a major just back from his first tour in Vietnam, took me on a sightseeing flight around southeastern Arizona. We did low-level flying most of the time, and I found that I could look directly into the sides of canyon walls as we blasted through. There is a straight railroad track that for miles crosses a huge dry playa that contains shallow water during the wet season. On that day, we noticed a long freight train starting to cross the playa, and the major decided that it would be fun to play chicken with the train. We circled around to the far side of the playa and descended to train engineer eye level above the rail track and headed directly for the lead engine. The last thing I saw as we approached the train was the engineer leaning out of the side window of the engine, waving his arms in an upward movement. We roared over the engine and banked away, laughing like fools. The major looked at me and said, "That was fun."

Some of the pilots got into trouble, as they would find a herd of cattle or horses and do a low-level pass over them, causing them to stampede. The local ranchers were not pleased, as they were trying to fatten up the cattle for market and the stampeding caused them to lose weight. Many times the ranchers would see a Mohawk approaching and fire shotguns at the planes. Finally, the ranchers had enough of these hijinks and met with the post commander, who promptly ordered anyone who flew to cease and desist with the animal harassment.

Time went by quickly, and soon my class of a dozen guys was issued orders, not for Germany or Korea, but to Mohawk units in Vietnam. I was the only one of the twelve who received orders to report to the 1st Cavalry Division; all of the other guys got assigned to the same Mohawk unit.

The next thing was a thirty-day leave, and then it was off to Oakland, California, for processing to depart for Vietnam.

2

Oakland, California

One of the Gateways to Vietnam

I was on my way to Vietnam via the Army post in Oakland, California. This was where you got ready to board a chartered 707 and leave for Vietnam. At this post, everyone received all of the shots necessary for keeping a person healthy and protected against numerous diseases prevalent in Vietnam. We stood in a long line in single file. On either side of us stood medical technicians, each of them holding a pneumatic gun–looking device with a hose attached to the grip portion of the gun. There were at least ten or a dozen of these medical people on each side of the aisle waiting for us to stand beside them and then move to the next position. The instructions were simple: When you got to a station, you would stand perfectly still as the technician pressed the injection gun against your arm and pulled the trigger. At that point, the gun would inject whatever vaccine they were administering into your arm. This injection occurred under great pressure, so it was imperative that you stand perfectly still because if you flinched, the nozzle moved against your skin, resulting in a nasty cut—almost like a razor or knife would do. These injections occurred on each of your arms at the same time. If you did flinch, you had to stand there while the technician gave you a second dose.

The technicians would play a game. They would purposely move the gun slightly against your arm as they pulled the trigger, causing a slight cut—not enough to warrant another dose but enough to start blood flowing. At the end of this gauntlet, there wasn't a single person who didn't have blood flowing down his arms and dripping off his fingers. There were technicians at the end of the shot process line who handed clean cloths to each guy, enabling us to clean up the blood; then additional technicians would place bandages on the guys who really flinched.

Since I was on flight status, I was required to have blood tests performed. The technique for an Army blood test is as follows: Stick your

15

left arm straight out in front of your body, make a fist, and then reach your right hand across your body and grasp your left bicep as tightly as you can; hold that position while a technician looks for a vein with his needle. After what seems much longer than necessary, you are told to release your right hand's grip and place a bandage on the needle extraction point on your left arm. For some reason, in a two-day time frame I probably had four or five blood tests performed. I don't know whether they kept losing my blood test vials or forgot to test for something or were just giving their new technicians some practice.

Finally, all the blood tests, physicals and shots were completed. The next step was to look for your name posted on the wall with a flight manifest number; when you found your name, you moved to a large auditorium and waited to be called to the tarmac for boarding.

The plane was a World Airways 707 that had been contracted with the government to bring us to Vietnam. The plane was full, of course, and we settled in for an extremely long flight. After about six or seven hours in the air, we were told to buckle up for landing. We all looked at each other, and several guys asked the flight attendants if we were landing in Vietnam. We were told that we were landing in Honolulu to top off our fuel supply. Everyone on the plane became very excited, as probably none of us had ever been to Hawaii. The 707 landed and taxied to a spot nowhere near the terminal. Everyone looked at each other and wondered out loud how we were supposed to get into the terminal from where we were parked. Then the front door of the airplane opened, and the most fantastic-smelling tropical air flowed into the plane. We sat there, inhaling deeply the fragrance of unknown flowers and fruits. However, as we started to unbuckle our seatbelts, several very large military policemen entered the airplane through the front door and loudly told everyone to sit down. No one was going to be allowed off the airplane. A few of the more senior officers stood up, as they felt entitled to be able to leave the airplane, but were firmly rebuffed by the MPs. I overheard one officer say to the MPs, "Do you see what rank I am?" "Yes, sir, I do; now please return to your seat, no one is exiting this airplane."

It seems that on some earlier flights that year, troops were allowed to exit their planes and told to stay inside the terminal. Unfortunately, a number of soldiers entered the terminal, immediately exited out the front door, got into cabs and never returned to the plane. They decided that Hawaii was a much better place than Vietnam and disappeared into the city, beaches and small towns to begin a new life. Therefore, regardless of our rank, we could only look out of our windows and breathe the wonderful air. Even though it was nighttime, we could see the lights of the high-rise buildings in Honolulu beckoning us to come and stay awhile.

With the refueling completed, we soon became airborne again, with the next stop the air base at Bien Hoa, Vietnam. The flight droned on for hours—lots and lots of hours. We slept, walked up and down the aisle, talked to our neighbors, read and slept some more. Finally, the pilot came on the intercom and advised us that we were approaching Vietnam and that the airplane would be blacked out for the approach to Bien Hoa. We looked out the windows but couldn't see much, as dawn was still a ways off. Suddenly, several of the guys on the opposite side of the airplane shouted, "Look at all those lightning flashes on the horizon!" A couple of the troops who were returning for a second tour of duty simply stated that those flashes were artillery firing or rounds impacting, not lightning (although there was lightning too). I made my way to a window and observed that every few seconds, there was a faraway flash of light on the horizon—and many times much closer than that.

The pilot came on the intercom and ordered everyone to sit down and securely fasten their seatbelts. There was a very good reason for firmly buckling ourselves in, which involved what the pilots had to do when landing at Bien Hoa. We made an abrupt dive toward the runway, not the long slow descent that commercial airplanes employ now. We performed that dive to avoid enemy fire and quickly approached the runway. After touching down, the plane moved rapidly on the ground so as not to attract mortar and rocket fire. As we came to a stop, several of the veterans who were returning to Vietnam said, "Gentlemen, this is not Hawaii—you will see what we mean when the doors open." We remained in our seats, not knowing what to expect, when suddenly the airplane doors opened. We were instantly assailed by the worst-smelling air that you can imagine. As we exited the plane, the heat, humidity and stench permeated everything. The only way to describe it is that it was a combination of jet fuel exhaust, rotting food, human excrement, sweat, dirty bodies, decaying fish and animals, and several other unidentifiable odors. The smell was overwhelming, and many of us placed our noses into the sleeves of our khaki shirts and tried to breathe through the fabric.

It was light enough now to see, but you couldn't see much because of the immense size of the airfield. There was constant noise from jet fighters taking off and artillery pieces shooting and men yelling at the top of their lungs, giving orders and directions. We were marched to a staging area and stood in formation, waiting for directions. As we stood there in the open in front of some bleachers, it started to rain; at first it was a light, very warm rain, but it soon started to rain quite hard. All of us immediately moved toward the cover of a building near us but were called back into formation. As we got soaked, we were told to get used to it, as this was just the beginning of many, many days of getting wet. The rain lasted long enough to thoroughly soak us; then the sun came out and baked us with heat and humidity. We were led to a mess hall for food and then to a barracks, where we were told to secure a bunk and put our duffle bag on it; then we proceeded outside to take a seat in the bleachers.

There were approximately 250 of us seated on the bleachers when a sergeant and several other NCOs addressed us. The ranking NCO said, "If I call your name, move to the green bleacher seats to your right." No one knew what was going on, so we all sat quietly while about fifty names were called. When all the names on his list were called, the rest of us were released to go back to the barracks. I was curious about why these guys had their names called, so I hung back and observed what happened next. I fumbled with my orders while watching the event unfold. Three different NCOs approached the green bleachers, and as I watched, the NCOs stood in front of the fifty or so guys and said, "Welcome to the United States Marine Corps." I moved away but was saying to myself, "Those guys are Army guys that had been drafted into the Army; how can they just be taken out of the Army and put into the Marine Corps?" As I was thinking those thoughts, I moved very quickly away from that group, as I did not want to look like I was interested in becoming a Marine—I had flying to do.

The next morning, I received my official orders assigning me to the 1st Cavalry Division's ASTA platoon. I was directed to a waiting bus filled with other guys who also were assigned to the 1st Cavalry. The bus's windows were covered with chicken wire to keep hand grenades from being tossed into the passenger area. We drove directly onto the tarmac and were directed to a waiting aircraft that would take us to the 1st Cavalry's headquarters located in An Khe. There we would spend a week getting trained in the ways of the Cavalry. I have already described some of the training we were given; then it was off to Phu Bai and the ASTA platoon and my bout with dysentery.

3

First Mission

Early June 1968—a typical thoroughly enjoyable day in I Corps, 104 degrees and humidity to match. Major Taylor said to me, "Are you ready for your first combat assault mission in Vietnam?" "Yes, sir," I replied. "Good, get your stuff and meet me on the flight line in five minutes."

I had been in Vietnam for about two weeks; the first week involved the usual processing in and the welcome to the 1st Cavalry Division in-country training program at a place somebody called Anne Kay (that is, An Khe—hey, I'm a New Englander, remember?), which included learning how to burn stuff from the latrines in barrels filled with diesel fuel, KP duty, and how to rappel out of a helicopter using a rope (which was demonstrated by a sergeant who grabbed a rope inside the hovering Huey, stood on the skid, lost his footing and grip on the rope, and promptly fell twenty feet into some waist-high grass—he had the wind knocked out of him but otherwise was OK).

Our rappelling session was quickly aborted when a lieutenant decided that we (approximately 20 FNGs—in other words, new guys) had better learn how to pull guard duty on the green line. That was OK with us, as it was much better than burning latrine stuff or KP duty. What we didn't know was that our section of the green line was directly in front of and below a battery of 155 and 175 mm howitzers. We were listening to a sergeant explain about bunkers and fields of fire, because not all of us were grunts (infantry), when he placed his hands over his ears. The next thing we knew, there was an explosion; we all had died and did not have any hearing left. When we got up off the ground and stopped shaking and checking our pants for stuff that didn't belong in them, the sergeant said, "Oh, that was only the 155s with an outgoing fire support mission; we are moving the green line farther away from them today—that's where you guys come in." Well, we and a company of grunts built new bunkers and moved the green line a respectable distance from the 155s. That night on the green line was uneventful except for the rain and bugs. I didn't sleep at all because I was sure that all the

19

VC and NVA troops in Vietnam were just beyond the concertina wire; they probably were but decided not to show themselves.

That morning, my name was called to get to the flight line and get a ride on a caribou or reindeer (an Army transport airplane) to another strange place called Weigh Phoo Bye (remember I am a New Englander), but when the plane landed I was sure that they had dropped me in the wrong place, because the sign said Hue (weigh) and Phu Bai—at least the second name sounded OK. I was told that I was in the correct place, and then I looked around the airfield and saw Mohawks—several of them— so I headed in that direction.

Mohawks are the Army's fixed-wing twin turboprop, short takeoff and landing combat surveillance aircraft made by Grumman, carrying a pilot and an observer, and it is equipped with a nose and belly camera and either a side-looking airborne radar system or an infrared target detection system. I have an information booklet given to me at the start of my Airborne Sensor School training at Fort Huachuca, published jointly by the U.S. Army and Grumman Aircraft, that details the Mohawk Surveillance System. It is comprehensive in describing the capabilities of the airplane and the camera and target detection systems, as well as the avionics and general information about the plane. My classmates and I devoured this information because we wanted and needed to know as much about this airplane as possible. I will list some of the general specifications and capabilities of the Mohawk: The plane was 41 feet long, with a wingspan of 48 feet for a side-looking airborne radar (SLAR) model "B" Mohawk and 42 feet for a "C" or "A" model. The "B" model weighed 13,749 pounds, while a "C" model was 13,186 pounds. The plane had an internal fuel tank with a capacity of 297 gallons and usually flew with two external fuel tanks attached to the underside of each wing, each tank holding 150 gallons. This fuel load gave the Mohawk a range of nearly 1,100 nautical miles with five and a half hours of flight time. The Mohawk had a maximum speed of 267 kilometers, but it could fly as slow as 72 kilometers before it stalled. The Mohawk could take off in 975–1,025 feet and needed 925 feet of runway to land and come to a stop.

I flew in the aircraft with the infrared system. In-cockpit communications were accomplished on my side of the cockpit via foot pedals. The foot pedal on the left side, when pressed and held down, enabled you to talk with the pilot, while the foot pedal on the right side of the floor connected you with all communication outside of the cockpit. The radios were located on a console off my left elbow, and I was within easy reach of all of them to change frequencies for communication with fire support bases, our platoon area, artillery units, other airplanes and the overall radar net surveillance group.

The SLAR was the AN/APS-94 system and had an in-cockpit display that showed "movers" on the screen; these movers were also captured on film that was later developed in a darkroom and then displayed on a light table for an imagery interpreter, who reported the findings to whoever had requested the mission. If faster action was required, as the movers were displayed on the in-cockpit screen, the targets would be reported and artillery or air strikes would occur.

I personally preferred flying in a Mohawk with the infrared system, the AN/AAS-14. This system displayed what was directly under the aircraft using heat differentiation to detect targets, displaying them as hot spots or cold spots on the terrain display indicators (TDIs). It was my job to look at the TDIs, compare the terrain displayed to my aerial map and determine what the hot or cold spots represented. The system would display terrain features, such as roads, trails, rivers and streams, and houses, but not images like vehicles or people. I would have to use my understanding of the system and my experiences to determine whether what I was seeing was anything that needed to be reported. (Later I will detail the procedure that I used to determine the validity of hot spots vis-à-vis potential targets.)

The camera systems included the KA-60 nose camera used for pantographic pictures (which I never used in Vietnam, but some units did) and the KA-30 belly camera (which I used often). The camera controls were located above the infrared system, and I could manually dial in the altitude and velocity, which would be displayed on the side margin of the developed film to assist the imagery interpreter in his analysis of the objects displayed. The system also had an automatic function that would set the camera focus for the altitude and speed of the aircraft. As with the nose camera, the belly camera contained a film canister that had to be removed from the airplane, brought to the darkroom, developed, hung to dry, and then placed on a light table for the imagery interpreter to review.

Many times after an interesting daytime photo mission, I would work with the imagery interpreter and point out things that I found worthy of further inspection. When I saw something of interest, I had a button to push that would put a mark in the margin of the film at the frame that I wanted to have examined with additional scrutiny. It was always fun after a mission, usually after a trail or stream recon, to see that altitude of the plane displayed in the margin of each frame. Both the belly camera and the infrared system could be used in filming a river or trail recon or could be used to make a mosaic of an area by making several parallel passes overhead. The film of each system, when developed, was cut into strips and taped together to form a map of the target area.

This new photo and/or infrared map could then be copied and distributed to units in the area to use in their upcoming operations.

The airplane was equipped with a relief tube that was simply a small funnel attached to plastic tubing that exited out of the bottom of the fuselage. This was used only when you couldn't hold it any longer and fortunately did not have the capability to help with any other bodily functions. I was careful about what I ate and drank before my missions, as I did not want to be flying for hours with discomfort. Likewise, I did not want to get sick in the airplane and create an unbearable situation with the heat and humidity. Fortunately, I never experienced any of the before-mentioned situations.

We had a drop chute in the cockpit that was a pipe big enough to easily hold a Coke can and supposedly used to drop messages in a container to a unit on the ground. We never did that, but on many occasions in the daytime we would bomb unsuspecting sampans with empty Coke cans. We would make a run and descend to just over them before we dropped the empty cans. Someone at one time suggested that we try doing that with hand grenades but promptly threw out that idea, as someone else said, "Imagine what would happen if somehow the grenade got jammed sideways in the drop chute and stayed there." We all decided that dropping empty Coke cans was the way to go.

Both target detection systems were used day and night, with the IR (infrared) system used at an altitude of 800–1,000 feet off the ground. Imagine flying at night with zero visibility in an area where the hills are 3,500 feet and higher and you are flying at 800 feet; you have to know exactly where you are at all times. The infrared gave me an instant display, similar to watching two 3-inch by 3-inch green television sets that were called terrain display indicators. Each of these TDIs was adjustable, allowing an observer to filter out features on one screen and leave those features visible on the other screen. For example, I would adjust the left screen to display only hot and cold spots and leave the right one to display whatever was on the ground directly beneath us. Between the TDIs and below them was an oscilloscope whose wave would peak for a strong hot spot reading and dip for a cold spot reading. With the TDIs set as I had them, and with the oscilloscope peaking and dipping, I could immediately get alerted to something on the ground that needed to be investigated.

When the oscilloscope peaked, I would look at the left TDI and see where the hot spot was located; then I would look at the right TDI and identify the hot spot on the ground, noting whether it was on a road or trail, in the water or in the jungle. I could then act on this information by alerting my pilot and pursuing a procedure that entailed contacting the closest fire support base to determine whether they had performed any recent missions that would cause small fires to remain burning. If their response was negative, we would then find out whether there were any friendlies working the area. If all was negative, we could safely assume that the hot spots were caused by VC or NVA cooking fires. At that point we would request a fire mission from a fire base that could have these coordinates in range. When the mission was complete, we would look for secondary explosions and request a 1st Cavalry blue team to check out the area in the morning.

The infrared technology would use heat differentiation to display potential targets as hot spots or cold spots—for example, a cluster of hot spots in the jungle not visible from the air would usually mean that there were people in the area using cooking fires, while cold spots could mean vehicles that had been sitting for a while with the engines off. The infrared system could be adjusted via filters to display only heat or hot spots that were in a specific temperature range. For example, in Vietnam, flying over triple canopy jungle, you wanted the system to be very sensitive to detect hot spots that could be cooking fires not visible from the air. It was even boasted that you could adjust the system to pick up a cigarette being lit in the jungle from an altitude of 1,000 feet or to pick up the heat generated by a Viet Cong or NVA soldier in the jungle scratching his ass. The hot spot in that instance would be minimal but would be presented on the TDIs, and if you were a good infrared technical observer, you would see the hot spot.

Mohawks were unarmed due to a directive initiated by the Air Force that the Army could not have armed fixed-wing aircraft. That was the job of the Air Force and the Navy. Consequently, all rocket and machine-gun pods were removed from all the Mohawks in Vietnam. In the earlier days of Vietnam, the Army did arm A model Mohawks with rocket pods and machine-gun pods that hung under the wing. The A model Mohawks had dual controls because they did not have the target systems (i.e., SLAR or infrared) installed. The A model's role was surveillance and close support, but, as I mentioned above, the Air Force complained about Army fixed-wing aircraft being armed, and the directive was issued to un-arm the Mohawks. The cockpit did have some armor panels in the floor that could absorb small-arms fire coming up from below the aircraft, and we also had armor at the base of our hatches to protect us from incoming rounds from the side.

The first guy whom I saw was evidently a crew chief, as he had most of his body inside the fuselage of a Mohawk. I asked whether these were ASTA Platoon 1st Cavalry OV-1s, and he pulled himself out of the airplane and pointed *way* down the airfield at a group of ragged tents full of holes, with three airplanes and a couple of bird dogs (small single-engine planes used for close infantry support to direct artillery fire) near some revetments. He said, "The Cav is down there." I thanked him and humped down the field to the tents, where I found the first sergeant and gave him my orders.

I was a TO (an enlisted man who has had over five months of specialized training to operate the target and camera systems in addition to navigating and operating the radios in the airplane; the TO is also known as a technical observer and will fly the plane on autopilot if something happens to the pilot). I was assigned to the 1st Cavalry Division Airmobile in the 11th General Support Aviation Company's ASTA (aerial surveillance and target acquisition) platoon. We had 6 OV-1 Mohawk aircraft, 4 pilots, 10 or 12 TOs, and 6 crew chiefs to take care of the airplanes; the rest of the platoon were support people who didn't fly, for a total strength of 30 people.

The sergeant pointed at a dilapidated tent (as all of them were, with shrapnel holes all over them) and said that was one of the TO tents. I walked into the tent; no one was there, but there were empty unused bunks everywhere, so I took one near the front opening of the tent. Over the next day or two I was able to get everything I needed for flying—my flight helmet, gloves, sunglasses, maps, and so on—and was ready to go. All I had left to do was meet the commanding officer (CO), Major Taylor. However, that night I went to sleep and woke with the stomachache to end all stomachaches. I ran for the latrine and just made it before dysentery took over my young life. I thought I would die; I wished I would die, but I survived. The next two or three days were notable because I had never been so sick. I cannot remember much of anything except one of the other TOs leaving cans of Coke near my head. I do remember that one day the first sergeant came into my tent because someone had told him there was a dead guy in the first TO tent. He walked in and almost passed out due to the aroma of the things dysentery does to you; then he said, "Who the hell are you?" I could barely answer him but pointed at my orders sitting in an empty ammo box. He looked at them and asked whether I had been sick since I checked in. I said, "Almost, except for the first day." By now, I was feeling a little better but weak as hell, and he was able to get some soup for me and more Coke to drink. I should have been hospitalized for dehydration and other things, but I wasn't and got better on my own. I learned an important lesson from my bout with dysentery: don't *ever* drink water in Vietnam. A few days later, I met Major Taylor, and that is when he asked whether I was ready to fly. I said yes, and he told me to get my helmet and my .38 revolver and meet him on the flight line in five minutes.

At the flight line, I asked Major Taylor whether he need me to plot the coordinates on my map for our mission. He smiled and shook his head and said that he knew where we were going and how to get there (and hopefully back). We were taking a C model Mohawk (one equipped with the infrared system) with the call sign "Black Knight 22" and were going on a daytime photo visual recon mission. It was mid-morning and, as I mentioned, brutally hot and humid. I was soaking wet as I sat in the cockpit wearing my survival vest and harness (we didn't wear flak vests), and I ran through the camera operation prior to takeoff. As we got airborne, I looked at the sand around Phu Bai and the ocean, and the realization struck me that here I was in Vietnam flying my first mission. As we flew, the major told me to look around, study my map and be able to tell where we were at a moment's notice, especially at night when we did IR missions, as that was what I wanted to do instead of SLAR missions. The major pointed to the north and identified the city of Hue (finally I realized that it was pronounced "weigh," not "hew"). He also pointed out the 1st Cavalry camp, Camp Evans, with what looked like hundreds of helicopters flying all over the place.

I was busy taking in the incredible scenery when I asked where we were headed; he looked at my map and pointed his finger at a location ahead of us. His finger was placed on the name "A Shau Valley." He asked whether I had ever heard of the place or of a nearby place called Khe Sanh; I nodded to him in the affirmative, and we were both silent for few moments. Major Taylor broke the silence when he said that we would make our first run from the south, with the prop and power levers at the max, and put the camera controls at auto altitude over velocity, as we would be coming in at 300 feet doing a visual of the airfield in the bottom of the valley to see whether we could see evidence of recent usage. Our assignment was to make two passes up the valley from the south. The first pass was just to the east of the center of the valley, flying over an old French airfield that the NVA (North Vietnamese Army) used. They even had a fake bomb crater on wheels that they would place in the center of the airstrip to fool us into thinking that the runway was unusable.

The next words the major said are with me today and forever: "When you see the tracers, let me know where they are coming from and which direction they are headed." I said, "When I see the tracers?" "You will absolutely see the tracers. If they are coming directly at us from the sides, we will be OK, but if they are coming up at us, or if they are leading us and are directed in front of us, let me know immediately." The major continued: "We have a slight advantage, as the NVA is used to shooting at helicopters and we are much faster than a helicopter, so it might take them a while to get a firm fix on us."

On our first run, we came in as fast as we could fly, with the belly camera taking frame after frame. I looked up from the camera controls and saw the Fourth of July: the air in front of us, beside us, above us and behind us was filled with green and red tracer rounds. I told Major Taylor what I saw on my side of the airplane while he watched his side and the front. I was busy telling him about the tracers coming up at us while keeping track of the ones coming down from the ridgetop. We completed our first pass without any hits and circled around for our stupid second pass, this time much closer to the hillside on our right—my side of the aircraft. We came in fast again, and immediately the air filled with tracers, but this time, as we were much closer to the hillside (probably one hundred yards), I saw something new: contrails coming toward us. I yelled "RPGs!" (rocket-propelled grenades) as the first went under my wing; the next was just behind us, and the third was leading us. At the same time that the RPGs came at us, many more tracers starting arching toward us, blocking our forward progress. Major Taylor looked at me and said, "We are out of here." He pulled back on the stick and turned right in the steepest banking turn that I have ever experienced (except for an additional two or three later in my tour) and headed over the ridge to the east. The ridgetop was very close to my side of the airplane, and as we came to the knife-edge ridgetop, I could look directly down (the plane was banking that sharply) into the faces of several NVA soldiers not fifty feet away, with their AK-47s pointed at us, and I could see the recoil from their rifles as they shot at us. The next second they were gone as we dove for the treetops and relative safety. We flew at tree-top level for many minutes

This is what you look like at 115 pounds after dysentery. I am on the left.

Me at my "home sweet home" in Phu Bai.

The controls for the infrared system, with hoods for the TDI screens and the oscilloscope. Note the power and prop levers mounted on the console with the rounded top.

with no words spoken; finally I said to Major Taylor, but more to myself, "This is going to be a long year."

It ended up being a very long year with many days and nights of continuous flying, no food except C-rations, beer in rusty cans, rocket and mortar attacks, and rats, lots and lots of rats—they enjoyed running amok in our tents, eating the food from our care packages from home and running up and down our bodies as we tried to sleep. Then there were bugs, snakes, bad food and no food, heat, unbearable humidity, monsoon rain, forever wet clothes, tents with holes in them, mortar and rocket attacks, sapper attacks and tigers.

I ended up flying more than 315 missions, probably adding up to over 1,000 hours of flight time. We got shot at during each and every mission. Sometimes the tracers were close to us, and sometimes the ground fire was from some very serious anti-aircraft weapons that nearly got us. Every one of our missions was a single ship mission; we never flew with another airplane for support. (We did, however, have Cobra gunships cover us at night during the UFO incident.) If we had a problem with the aircraft, we could only hope that the plane was still flyable enough to make it to an airstrip or, if not, that our Martin-Baker ejection seats would perform as expected and parachute us safely to the ground.

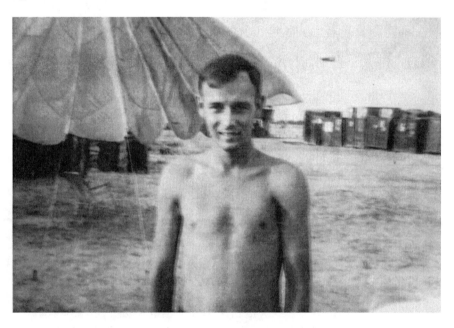

Me, shortly after recovering from dysentery.

I have many more stories, but this was the first mission; others are equally intense (if not more so). Ask me about being chased by Migs, chasing a UFO, experiencing an airplane on fire, being at a fire support base under rocket and mortar attack while we were on the runway, getting caught in a B-52 bombing strike, celebrating New Year's Eve with a squad of seriously drunk Aussie grunts, and on and on ... oh yes, there was also the Marines throwing CS gas canisters into our tents from one of their bars located next to our area across some concertina wire for fun—we got even!!!! Don't mess with 1st Cavalry Division troopers.

4

The Outhouse Transaction

We had a platoon first sergeant who was a typical first sergeant, which meant that he was a wheeler/dealer. One day in midsummer he advised us that he had acquired a brand new portable outhouse; from whom or where he did not say. He did inform us that anyone who wanted to volunteer for a road trip could come with him via deuce and a half truck for a journey north on Highway 1. The destination was a Navy supply depot on the coast just south of the ancient city of Hue. All we had to do was load the outhouse onto the bed of the truck, grab our weapons and climb aboard. The reason for the trip was to deliver the outhouse to the Navy for an undisclosed trade of goods. Why the Navy wanted an outhouse was beyond my reasoning, as when we arrived at the depot, we found that the naval personnel had indoor showers with hot water and flush toilets. (Maybe they wanted it for their beach so that they wouldn't have to leave their beach blankets for so long when nature called.)

Seven or eight of us, both flying and non-flying troops, agreed to go on the trip. We were to provide security for this delivery. We were a one-truck convoy, which was very unusual and dangerous, as daily ambushes occurred on Highway 1 to truck convoys carrying supplies. These convoys always had armed jeep escorts. As we progressed north, we began to feel increasingly uneasy, as there were no other vehicles (military or civilian) on the highway. We had three people in the cab of the truck, while the rest of us rode in the truck bed with the outhouse. A plan ran through my mind that if we got hit, I could use the outhouse for cover.

As I mentioned, we were a single-truck convoy, and as we rounded a bend, we heard heavy machine-gun fire ahead of us. We slowed, and all of us went on high alert, scanning the bushes on either side of the road next to us and ahead of us. Two or three hundred yards beyond our position the highway curved to the right and then left. As we neared the curve, we heard another short burst of machine-gun fire; then all was quiet. We rounded the next curve and found a small convoy of three trucks and two MP jeeps as escorts. These jeeps were equipped with quad .50-caliber machine guns positioned behind the driver and passenger seats. On the side of the road were the bodies of several Viet Cong soldiers who had made the mistake of ambushing the three trucks. The ambushers had let the lead MP jeep pass before they started firing at the trucks, not realizing that a second MP jeep was sandwiched between the trucks. That second jeep ruined their ambush plans. The MPs waved us through but couldn't believe we didn't have an escort. If we had been five minutes or less early, we would have been the Viet Cong's target and the outcome substantially different.

We stayed hyper alert until we reached the outskirts of the city of Hue. This city was the ancient Vietnamese capital and spectacular in its beauty. The colonial French influence was everywhere, with a combination of European and Asian architecture in the buildings, street layout and parks. Unfortunately, a large part of the city was destroyed during the Tet offensive, which had occurred a few months earlier during the Lunar New Year. Some of the heaviest and most intense battles of the entire war occurred during the Tet offensive, with incredible losses of civilians and soldiers on both sides.

We continued past Hue to the large Navy support base located south of Hue on the coast. The naval installation was quite large and very busy, with supply ships being unloaded while others waited offshore. Because we lived in tents with holes in them, we were shocked to see real buildings with walls and roofs, indoor plumbing and air conditioning. We were further shocked to see television sets, a laundry, and a PX (or BX, as it is referred to in the Navy).

When we arrived at our outhouse exchange point, it was lunchtime, and we were invited to have lunch at the naval mess hall. As we entered the mess hall, which was packed with sailors, the entire place became deathly quiet as hundreds of eyes focused on us. We were, after all, 1st Cavalry troopers and wore our normal attire for daily life, which included a helmet, flak vest, M-16 rifle with at least two bandoliers of ammunition, frag grenades hanging from our vests, and dirty, rumpled jungle fatigues. We all had several days' worth of beard growth and probably smelled as bad as we looked. We stood transfixed as several hundred sailors stared at us, not believing their eyes. Here in their mess hall stood eight real live soldiers, warriors, and the bravest of the brave (at least that's what we thought they were thinking; in reality, they were probably wondering how they could get us smelly, unkempt excuses for military people out of their mess hall).

The mess hall was a wondrous place to behold: the delicious odors from the food, the vast amount of all kinds of different food available—all you had to do was take a tray and plate and help your-self. No powdered eggs or terrible-smelling mystery meat; they had real milk from real cows, plus T-bone steak from the barbecue, cooked as you liked—you could even have two if you wanted. The vegetables were fresh, the fruit ripe and sweet. We didn't know what to do, so we stood there staring, holding up the line until someone behind us said, "What is the matter with you guys? It's only food; now move the line." For a group of guys that lived on C-rations and powdered junk, this offering of food was more than a banquet; it was a dream come true. We ate and then ate some more; we even had several choices of dessert, from ice cream to pudding and pies and cake. We each drank about a gallon of fresh milk and then waddled outside to the beach. We went swimming in the ocean and sat or laid in the shade until the first sergeant rushed out to us and said that we had to get going *now*, as we had to get back to our area in Phu Bai before dark. We quickly thanked our Navy friends, grabbed our stuff (and several doggie bags of food), and climbed onto our truck.

In the back of the truck, we found two thirty- or forty-pound crates full of frozen steaks. The cartons were covered with blankets to help pre-serve the cold temperature. We also discovered a couple of cases full of two distinguished gentlemen—namely, Jim Beam and Jack Daniels. Our first sergeant certainly knew how to make a great deal. A new outhouse that we didn't need became two cases of T-bone steaks and two cases of bourbon and whiskey.

We entered Highway 1 and headed south, making very good time—those of us riding in the back of the truck had to almost strap ourselves in to keep from becoming airborne when the truck rounded bends in the road. Due to the earlier attempted ambush, we went on high alert as soon as we merged onto Highway 1 and headed south toward Phu Bai. It was now late afternoon, and soon the sun would be going down—the perfect time for an ambush. The sergeant told us to be ready for anything because we were again traveling without an escort. Everyone on that truck studied every bush and clump of grass along that road, expect-ing shots directed at us. I constantly turned around to look behind us, concerned that a VC unit would wait until we passed and then launch an RPG at us. Maybe taking a road trip and delivering an outhouse to the Navy was not such a good idea after all. We watched the setting sun with growing concern, thinking that we would still be on the road in the darkness, but as that thought crossed our minds and we verbalized the potential consequences, an airplane buzzed over our heads on short final into Phu Bai.

Ten minutes later, we pulled into our platoon area and unloaded our cartons and crates, bringing them into the first sergeant's tent, where he carefully covered his treasures with blankets. With everything secured, we headed to our club for a well-deserved beer, while the sergeant proceeded to welcome his new friends, Mr. Beam and Mr. Daniels, to his own private party. We would feast on those T-bone steaks when they thawed.

The first sergeant was also an expert on getting us to participate in routine "midnight requisitions" from our neighboring Marine Corps supply depot. But that is another story....

5

The Rats versus McMann

Midsummer, Phu Bai, Republic of South Vietnam, approximately 9:00 p.m. (2100 hours military time): I had just vanquished a mosquito that somehow had gotten inside my mosquito netting, which had been buzzing in my ears for ten minutes. I finally, after many nights and days of flying, was going to get a full night's sleep. I had been assigned to fly infrared target missions later that night and early morning with Major Taylor, but the missions were scrubbed due to increasingly violent weather in our target areas.

As I closed my eyes, someone burst into my tent, shining a flashlight in my eyes. "Pettis, I need to borrow your .38" (my .38 was a Smith & Wesson six-shot revolver that I carried when I flew as well as everywhere else). This request was made by McMann, an OV-1 Mohawk crew chief whose airplane I flew in most often. McMann was a great kidder with a good sense of humor and quick wit, and he was usually intelligent. He would climb up to the cockpit as I was connecting my harness and seatbelt and say, "Things were hectic today and I can't remember if I fully torqued the main hydraulic connection, but don't worry—if it does start to leak, you will still have an hour or two before the aircraft controls start to seize." I would look at him and say, "Don't tell me this stuff; tell the major—he's flying this thing." McMann would then climb down from the cockpit and look up at me, grin, and give me the peace sign. He would then grab a fire extinguisher and wait while we started the plane's two turboprop engines, just in case there was a hydraulic leak that would immediately lead to a fire.

"McMann, why do you want to borrow my .38?" He replied, "I have three huge rats cornered near the flight line, and my M-16 is too loud and powerful. I think that these rats are the same ones that got into the care package that I just received tonight from home and ate everything that was in it, including the wrappers—not a crumb left for me." We had such a rat problem (as did all of Vietnam) that you sometimes wondered if the rats would band together and pull you off your bunk. They

34

were everywhere and into everything; you couldn't go to the latrine or take a shower without seeing a rat. McMann was almost in tears as he recounted his care package story.

"McMann, you said that you had the rats cornered. How can that be if they are near the flight line and you are here bothering me when I'm trying to sleep?" "Oh, I left them a piece of gum, so I'm sure that they are still there." Finally I said, "If I let you borrow the gun, will you put it back and leave me alone?" "Yes, thank you," he said and took my revolver out of my gun case and started to leave. "Hey, McMann, it's not loaded; you probably want to grab some bullets." He took a handful of bullets and hurried out of my tent.

I had just laid back in my bunk, free from pesky mosquitos and soaked with sweat, and tried to imagine being somewhere else. BANG, BANG, BANG, BANG, BANG, BANG. I jumped out of my bunk; pulled on my pants, boots, flak jacket and helmet; and ran out of my tent. The shooting was close, *very* close to my tent, as well as the major's quarters and the administration tent. As I ran out of my tent, I realized that I was unarmed, but the major and our three other pilots came scrambling out of their living quarters (a metal CONEX container with a small A/C unit powered by a generator), waving their pistols and revolvers and aiming in the direction the shots came from. At the same time that all this was happening, our hero McMann came running up to us yelling, "I think I hit one of them, but the others were quick, so I chased them up here firing as I ran after them."

The major, an incredibly refined, soft-spoken gentleman from Arkansas, who neither swore nor ever got flustered or raised his voice, found his vocal cords that evening: "McMann, who did you shoot, are there more of them, are they sappers trying to blow up our airplanes, where did they go?" "McMann, we almost shot you; all we saw was someone running toward us with a gun and flashlight. What in heck [yes, he said heck] are you doing?" McMann was out of breath after chasing the thieving rats, but he managed to reply, "I was chasing and shooting rats, sir—the rats that ate my care package contents tonight." The major stood stock still at McMann's explanation, noticing for the first time the .38 Smith & Wesson revolver in his hand. "Where did you get the revolver?" I jumped in at that time and said, "I let him borrow it to shoot some rats near the flight line, whom he was sure ate his care package goodies." The major had calmed down, realizing that we were not under attack, and looked at McMann, whom he told to return the revolver to me, and then he turned to me with these words: "Do not ever loan your weapon to him again." Then to McMann: "Please report to me first thing in the morning." We all quickly left the area and headed to our tents and bed.

The rats that McMann had chased had regrouped or called for rein-forcements and ran amuck around our platoon area, knowing that more care packages could be found.

I recall seeing McMann the next morning with a bucket and entrenching tool, combing the company area, the pilots' CONEX con-tainer perimeter and the weeds near the flight line for rat feces, which he would then take a quarter mile away and bury. McMann never went rat shooting again, and I flew that morning with the major, who didn't say a word about the incident. (There is another McMann story that does not involve rats or shooting, but rather his uncanny knack for wheeling and dealing, which has to do hooches, fans and mattresses—see Chapter 17)

6

A Typical Day

*There Was No Such Thing; Sometimes
They Don't Miss Their Target*

A day that involved flying (which was almost every day) started at
10:00 p.m. (or 2200 hours) with a briefing in the ops (operations) tent to
look at our flight and target assignments. I always flew IR (infrared) missions because I enjoyed the real-time images and low-level flying, even
at night. We received our targets directly from 1st Cavalry headquarters,
which meant that the Cavalry was going to do something very soon after
seeing our film and discussing our debriefing. Usually our IR missions
comprised several rectangular-shaped target areas located throughout I Corps (i.e., near the DMZ and westward toward Laos). We were
assigned target areas along rivers, trails and roads, in valleys and along
ridgelines. Sometimes we would fly "feet wet," over the ocean along the
shoreline, to see whether there was any boat activity along the shore or
near any of the many islands located just offshore. I plotted our target
areas on my map prior to taking off. The map was covered with a thin
clear plastic coating that would allow me to make notes using a grease
pencil. Radio call signs and radio frequencies for fire support bases and
other places with a runway were noted on the map. Other notes, including weather information and specific instructions, were also present
on the map. During a daytime visual reconnaissance mission, I would
use the grease pencil to mark coordinates of targets or other interesting things that we saw as we flew the mission. The best part about using
a grease pencil on acetate was that you could easily remove anything
you had written with a cloth, sometimes using cigarette ash to assist in
removing any stubborn grease pencil markings.

One time we were flying feet wet during the day, using the belly
camera and the infrared system together, when the infrared system indicated that we were over land; we were at least a mile offshore, but the
system clearly showed what looked like land. I peered out the window

and asked my pilot to look at the system, and he was as shocked as I was to see what appeared to be land. The infrared system had discovered an offshore reef that had not been noted on our maps. We contacted the Navy and advised them of what we had discovered. We gave them the coordinates and looked for more hidden reefs as we headed for our search areas. The Navy called us back, as they had sent out a plane of their own and confirmed our reef find. I wondered whether they would name it after us.

After our briefing and target assignments, the pilot and I would meet at our airplane and do a preflight check to look for any hydraulic leaks or damage to any part of the airplane that hadn't been noticed before. We also checked our fuel supply, especially our under-wing mounted auxiliary fuel tanks (one under each wing) that looked identical to bombs, which gave us an extended range and flight time. If we had time, we would go to the 131st Aviation Company's mess hall for a quick bite of midnight chow. If we didn't have time, we would grab a package of C-rations and find something edible.

As we taxied to the runway, I would turn on my infrared system to let it warm up and check for any faults before we became airborne, as you didn't want to wait until you were in the air to turn on the system, find a fault and then have to land to either try to repair the system or change airplanes. A typical IR mission would take all night, flying at 800–1,000 feet. This was concerning, as the terrain around us had 3,000-foot mountains, so we had to be alert and know where we were at all times. This knowledge was vitally important if the weather turned bad.

The infrared system used real-time heat differentiation to display hot spots and cold spots on my screens. I had two small green display screens called terrain display indicators (TDIs) with hoods on the top to limit the amount of light in the cockpit; between and below these two screens was an oscilloscope with a wave that would peak for a hot spot and dip for a cold spot. The movement of the oscilloscope wave would get your attention to quickly look at the TDIs to see what was displayed on the ground while looking at the map in your lap. All this happened simultaneously. If a hot spot was displayed, you looked out the cockpit window for a visual confirmation. The system would display the ground features below the aircraft, so it was easy to tell whether the hot spot was on a road, on a trail, in a river or simply in the jungle. I would set the contrast on the left TDI to wash out terrain features, causing any hot spots or cold spots to stand out, catching your peripheral vision. When that occurred, you looked at the right TDI to identify exactly where the potential target was located. A quick glance at the map that was always open on your lap would positively locate the target. The map was accurate in that you could see whether the target (or targets) was on a road, trail, body of water or jungle.

If, for example, a random group of hot spots suddenly appeared on the screens and were not visible from the cockpit, we would immediately contact the nearest fire support base and ask whether they had any recent fire missions in that area that could account for small fires still burning. Next we would ascertain whether there were any friendlies in the area that might be using small, covered fires. If there were no recent artillery missions and no friendlies in the area, we would assume that these hot spots were small cooking fires from a group of NVA soldiers. At that time we would call in an artillery strike to the coordinates that I identified and have a 1st Cavalry blue team (infantry squad) investigate the area in the morning. It was always interesting to try to explain to an artillery officer why we wanted a fire mission on a group of hot spots. This was the standard procedure whenever we found targets. Sometimes it was much easier to determine who was down there when tracers would come up at us from the jungle.

After completing our assigned target areas just before dawn, we were usually low on fuel and returned to base to refuel, run for the latrine and perhaps dig into the C-rations again, as there was no time to visit the mess hall. We used the same airplane, only this time for a daytime visual and camera recon. The camera would take frame after frame until you turned it off. In the margins of each frame, certain information was displayed to assist the imagery interpreter. I would on many occasions work with the interpreter, especially if we saw anything interesting during our flight. Many of these photo/VR (visual recon) missions were done at extreme low-altitude levels. It was not unusual to read on the film margins our altitude readouts as sixty feet, seventy-five feet, and so forth. We actually had to dodge around the taller trees in front of us when doing riverside trail recons. We could (and often did) perform several of these daytime missions a day. There were many times that I flew around the clock two or three days in a row.

I returned from a photo/VR mission one afternoon to find several guys playing volleyball in the sand. I joined them; as tired as I was, it was much too hot to try to sleep in the tent. As the ball was served, a shrieking rattling noise came in over our heads as a 122 mm rocket and several of its friends roared into sight. There was a bunker fairly close to us, and we all ran for it while yelling "Incoming!" I was on the far side of the bunker and was next to last getting inside. We were all delayed getting into the bunker because one of the guys who was an extreme short-timer had moved into it and blocked most of the entrance with his stuff. Just as I was ducking through the opening, something hit me on the side of my head above my left ear; it didn't hurt, but I was high on adrenaline. As I fully entered the bunker, our resident bunkerite yelled, "You're hit!" I put my hand to my head and felt something wet, and as I pulled my hand away, it was covered with blood. The rocket and mortar attack didn't last long, so I left the bunker and went to our shower/washroom and washed the blood away, but there was a small cut that was still bleeding. I went to our ops tent, and the platoon clerk got out the first aid kit and gave me some antiseptic and a large bandage. That was it. I went back to the bunker, and several feet from where I had entered it, I found a piece of shrapnel in the sand with a small amount of blood on it. It had evidently exhausted almost all of its energy when it glanced off my head.

It was now my turn to get even with the care package–devouring rats. I knew from McMann's experience that I couldn't take my .38 and chase rats around inside or outside my tent—I had to think of something else. What if I developed a .38-caliber rat round that was safe to use in the tent and near it outside? I thought for a bit and decided that I would try this plan. I took a .38-caliber bullet and used pliers to pull out the lead, being careful not to dump out the gunpowder. I then took a candle, lit it and, being very careful, dripped melted wax in the jacket where the lead had been. I was concerned that maybe the hot wax would ignite the gunpowder, so I performed the dripping wax routine with shields between me and the bullet. Everything went well, with no gunpowder explosion.

Now it was time to test the effectiveness of my wax rat round. I checked the back of the tent; all that was there were 55-gallon drums full of sand topped by several rows of sandbags to protect us from rockets and mortars, so that area could stop even an M-16 round. I fully expected the canvas wall of the tent to stop the wax round and backed up fifteen or twenty feet and fired the wax round, aiming about two feet off the floor. The revolver made a slight popping noise, and the wax round tore through the canvas tent wall and embedded itself five inches into a sandbag.

I made six more wax rat rounds and that night waited for the despised uninvited guests to appear to raid my care package, looking for crumbs. I placed a piece of cracker on the floor near the edge and waited. I could hear the rats scrambling around under the wooden floor of the tent, and several times they climbed up onto the tent floor, noticed me and disappeared before I could react. I made the mistake of standing on the floor instead of sitting on my bunk, but even sitting quietly on my bunk, the wary rats would notice me and duck back under the floor. Now was the time for some Yankee ingenuity. The rats could see me immediately if I was standing or sitting. I reasoned that I needed to get down to their level, so I lay down on the floor, rested the butt of the .38 on the floor and sighted in on the spot at the edge of the wooden tent floor where they always appeared. "Now," I thought, "I have the advantage." I cocked the .38 and waited quietly, barely breathing, when suddenly I saw movement. The rat was quick, but not as quick as I was as I squeezed the trigger. The revolver made a popping noise, and I inched over to the edge of the floor and, flashing my red-lensed flashlight over the edge, discovered a very dead large rat.

I retreated on my stomach back to my ambush spot and waited for the next victim. I didn't have to wait long before I saw movement again at the edge of the floor, and I squeezed the trigger. This time I saw the rat somersault backward and, upon a cursory examination, found the second rat lying dead next to the first one. I settled back to my spot on the floor and soon noticed more movement; again the rat round found its mark. One more rat tried his luck for care package goodies, only to find a rat round instead. Four down, four billion to go!

In the morning, before the temperature got crazy, I had the unpleasant task of disposing of those four dead rats. I took my entrenching tool and, being careful not to touch those rats, placed them in a bucket and gave them a burial without ceremony somewhere in the sand, far away from our platoon area. However, my night flying schedule did not allow me the time to go on another rat safari in my tent.

An incredibly sad day came when one of our Mohawk aircraft claimed another one of us. It happened on a very dark night to one of the senior TOs. He was on an IR mission and must not have turned the system on to test it until they were airborne. He must have tested the IR film mode and forgotten to turn it off, thereby causing the system to continuously operate, taking frame after frame, just like the belly camera does. With the system recording the images during the flight to the first target area, the film canister was running low on film. When the first target area was completed, the TO turned off the recording toggle switch. As they started the second target area, the system fault illuminated, signifying an empty film canister. These target areas were considered critical, so the pilot had no choice but to return to base for a fresh film canister. There are two canisters in the IR system: one is filled with fresh film, and the second is the take-up spool that contains the images. Each canister is about the size of a quart container of oil. In technical observer school, we were blindfolded and had to become proficient in reloading the film from the new canister into the take-up canister. The new film was inserted under and over various rollers until it reached the take-up canister into which the film was inserted and firmly attached to the core spool inside the canister. Then you had to test the film by turning a knob on the take-up spool and ensuring that film was being pulled from the full canister and properly taken up and loaded in the other canister. All this had to be done with your eyes closed or blindfolded, as any light would immediately expose the film, making it useless.

The procedure in place at the time was for the TO who was flying the mission, upon landing, to exit the aircraft, unload the full take-up canister, bring it to the darkroom for processing, take a fresh canister to the plane, remove the IR cover and thread the new film into the take-up canister. This night, however, things went terribly wrong, as the TO was tired (it was the middle of the night or very early morning), and he forgot the cardinal rule of flying—never approach an aircraft from the front. Both engines were operating as he climbed down from the cockpit, and, instead of walking away from the engine on his side of the plane and going to the end of the wing, and then around the tail and up along the pilot's side of the fuselage to the IR access port (which was under the wing), he climbed down from the cockpit and walked around the nose of the plane, directly into the spinning propeller. He was wearing his flight helmet, which the first of the three blades of the propeller removed, while the other two finished the job.

We changed the procedure the next day, and I was the first to use the new practice, which stipulated that if a plane returned for a film canister change, a TO who was not flying would be summoned to meet the airplane, replace the film, and remove the full canister and bring it to the darkroom. The flying TO would not exit the airplane, instead waiting for the other TO to take care of refreshing the film.

Shortly after that experience, I was called upon to replenish the canisters. Fully aware of what had happened, I approached the idling airplane from the rear, ducked under the wing, accessed the IR unit, threaded the new film and checked the take-up spool for correct operation. While I was doing this, I was extremely cognizant of the fact that a three-bladed turboprop was spinning just off my left shoulder. The infrared access door was located on the pilot's side of the airplane on the side of the fuselage, just under the leading edge of the wing and very close to the spinning propeller. I realized that if I extended my left arm from where I was standing, I probably could have touched the propeller blades. Therefore, I kept my arms down and concentrated on threading the new film around, under and through the take-up rollers and then into the take-up spool. Remember that I could not use a flashlight, as exposing the film to light would render it useless, so I had to do everything by memory, experience and feel.

After I completed the correct threading of the new film into the take-up spool and checked that the take-up was working properly, I proceeded along the fuselage to the rear of the plane, went around the tail and out to the end of the wing, then around that, and finally got even with the nose camera and approached the pilot's hatch from the front. As I got near the hatch and lowered the telescoping step, I couldn't believe how close I was to the propeller. I stood on the step and pulled myself up to the open hatch to speak with the pilot (who was a captain I enjoyed flying with) and informed him that the IR system was refilled with new film and he was good to go. He told me to be careful as I got down from his hatch and pushed the telescoping step back into the fuselage. I stood at the base of the step for a second and cleared my head again and looked at the spinning propeller that was so close to my body. I hoped that a gust of wind would not suddenly push me in the wrong direction; then I put my hand on the fuselage and walked forward to the nose of the plane and continued straight ahead until I was at least a hundred feet from the airplane. I then looked back at the plane and walked away and back to bed.

The thing you had to remember was to fully awaken yourself after being roused out of a sound sleep before you attempted to do anything around the airplane. I would always completely clear my head, shake out the cobwebs and focus on what I was doing and what needed to be done.

We discovered through various sources that a Mohawk crewmember had a $5,000 bounty placed on him by the Viet Cong, NVA, Chinese, Russians or whomever. The reason for the bounty was that with our infrared radar, we could find them on the ground at night, and with the side-looking radar, we could see traffic moving on the trails, especially the Ho Chi Minh Trail in Laos. We tried not to imagine the treatment we would receive if we ever punched out of the plane and were captured. Several of us discussed this situation and came up with few viable survival scenarios. If we were injured when we punched out and the ejection seat performed properly, we would land on the ground via parachute and most likely end up hanging up in the trees. The jungle here was triple canopy, and the larger trees were at least 125 feet tall. If you were injured and stuck in the trees and it was pitch black, you couldn't do much until dawn. If you could get out of the tree and your injuries were not too bad, you would have to watch for patrols looking for you and try to avoid them until you were rescued. In addition, you would not have food or water. If you were discovered and could try to protect yourself, the general consensus was to make a last stand and keep one bullet in reserve as a way of not getting captured. Not a pretty picture, but one that we had to consider.

We would sit around drinking and discussing scenarios for survival if we ever did have to punch out of the plane. We talked about what we would do if we punched out and landed in the ocean or in a river or even a rice paddy. We wore survival vests when we flew that contained signaling items and first aid items but no food or water. The vest had a zipper pocket that held our .38 revolver or a .45-caliber pistol. I always carried extra ammunition in my leg pockets. We would talk about landing in the jungle and what survival tricks could be used to evade capture until we could be rescued. We talked about the pros and cons of moving at night versus moving in the daylight and how to camouflage ourselves to blend in with the jungle.

We also discussed whether to engage the enemy if we saw them first. One idea was to shoot first as long as there were only two or three men in the patrol, to take them by surprise and take their weapons (an AK-47 with a 30-round magazine beats six or eight shots from a handgun every time). These troops, if we got them first, might also have some food and water that we could use. That was one scenario that was discussed; another was to hide until the patrol moved away. It came down to your individual judgment regarding whether you thought that you could take out two or three people before one of them got you.

The decision of whether to move at night was fairly simple. Unless you knew exactly where you were, and could see a safe destination, your best bet was to find a thick brushy place to hide and spend the night. Several guys noted that they would hide inside a large bush, but the rest of us didn't like the idea of spending the night on the ground for several reasons. First, an enemy night patrol could find you; second, there were lots of crawly creatures on the ground, such as snakes, pythons, fleas, spiders, and so on, as well as large four-legged things that would eat you. I reasoned that finding a good tree and climbing it until I found a suitable place in the branches of the tree to spend the night was the best choice. Of course, there would be plenty of mosquitos, but I reasoned that mosquito bites would be the least of my worries.

Luckily, none of us had to deal with any of these scenarios, as none of us had to eject from an airplane. There was a TO from another Mohawk company who ejected twice, the first time landing in the Saigon River and the second time landing in a rice paddy near the Cambodian border. He and the pilot were rescued quickly from the rice paddy. The TO told me that he had borrowed a friend's brand new 35 mm SLR Nikon camera to take pictures during his mission. The weather that day was clear and sunny, perfect for taking pictures—that is, until his plane got hit by ground fire and decided that it did not want to fly any longer. When the decision was made to punch out, my friend looked at his buddy's brand new camera, which was hanging around his neck by the strap, and decided that the camera was going with him out of the airplane. He told me that he unbuckled the parachute harness on his chest, put the camera inside the harness straps and buckled the harness again with the camera held firmly in place against his chest. He then ejected from the plane; the seat fired correctly, and he separated from it and found himself floating to earth toward a rice paddy full of water. He did a perfect stand-up landing, released the parachute harness and noticed his pilot descending toward the same rice paddy. Remembering the camera around his neck, my friend picked it up and took several photos of his pilot as he landed in the paddy. They had sent out a mayday prior to punching out, giving their heading and location, and a Huey quickly arrived and pulled them out of the rice paddy. My friend never mentioned much about his first experience punching out except the pilot had jettisoned the wing drop tanks prior to ejecting from the plane and my friend landed close to one that was floating in the river; he swam to it and hung onto the tank until he was rescued. I don't know what happened to the pilot, and I can't remember whether my friend ever told me. He probably did tell me what happened, but I don't want to give any information that could be false.

Another day Mr. Williams and I walked to the flight line together, discussing our bad fortune to be assigned this particular bird for a visual recon flight. Our C model infrared-equipped Mohawks were already being used, and since Mr. Williams was the low-ranking pilot, he was left with this beast for our mission. This ship was a B model SLAR (side-looking airborne radar) Mohawk that under the best of conditions was underpowered and handled like a dump truck. Even under ideal flying conditions, this thing used all the runway it could find just to get airborne. Once in the air, the airplane eventually reached altitude and would fly in a straight and level line until it was forced to turn. This was fine for SLAR missions, when all you did was fly at a specific altitude in a straight line and then turn in the opposite direction and fly until you fell asleep. This airplane (and I call it an airplane only because it would eventually leave the ground) did not like to dive or make abrupt movements necessary to avoid incoming tracers.

We did our preflight check and unfortunately could not find anything amiss that we would determine serious enough to give the plane a red X, signifying it was not safe to fly. We climbed into the cockpit, fastened our seatbelts and connected our parachute harnesses, and waited while the crew chief got the fire extinguishers and while the engines, one at a time, were cranked. This was the time for a hot start, as we both said out loud, but no—the damn engine on the pilot's side fired up nicely, then the engine on my side started to crank, and it, too, started. We were on our way, my map in my lap, and as we continued down the taxiway, we looked at each other and shrugged "OK, let's do this thing." I called out, "Hot and locked," as I armed my ejection seat and locked the hatch release lever in place; Mr. Williams said, "Hot and locked," and we were cleared onto the active runway.

It was 8:00 a.m., and the weather was hot and humid but clear, with little wind, as we sat at the end of the runway, did final checks, ran up the engines, feathered the propellers and received final clearance from the tower for takeoff. We double-checked our ejection seats and harnesses and powered up, with the brakes holding us in place. The prop levers were maxed, our flaps were set, and then the power levers were pushed all the way forward; the brakes were released, and off we went rumbling down the runway—no, I'm wrong, it *lumbered* down the runway, gathering speed like it was being pushed by a high school linesman. All we could do was sit and wait until we reached rotation speed as we watched the end of the runway approach, with the Phu Bai sand getting closer and closer. Finally, the nose came up, and Mr. Williams yelled to me to put the gear up. I pushed the landing gear lever forward and watched as my main gear disappeared into its bay in the wing. Mr. Williams all this time was holding the power levers to the maximum level with one hand, holding onto the stick with the other while watching the instruments. He didn't dare pull back on the stick very much, as he didn't want to bleed off air speed. We slowly climbed out over the ocean and breathed a sigh of relief as the airplane remembered that it could indeed fly.

We considered for a moment declaring a mayday and punching out over the shallow ocean water, putting this airplane out of its misery before it killed someone, but that would involve too much paperwork, and what if the ejection seats didn't work properly and we ended up hitting the ocean still strapped to our seats? We decided to do our mission but were very careful where we went and how low we flew.

All went well for a few hours until we received a radio call directing us to land at a nearby fire support base and meet with the base commanding officer. We contacted the fire support base about landing there and were told that there was no problem for us, as a C-130 took off from there recently. We circled the base and came in for a landing. That worked out OK, and we parked the airplane off the runway at the end nearest the headquarters bunker. The CO handed us a sealed envelope that he said needed to be delivered as soon as possible to the 1st Cavalry Headquarters at Camp Evans. At this point, we had used enough fuel to make us lighter and the runway was in good shape, but they were incorrect when they said that a C-130 had taken off from there—it was actually a C-123 equipped with JATO assists mounted to the sides of the fuselage behind the wings. (JATOs were two small jet engines, one attached to each side of the fuselage, that were activated on takeoff to allow the plane to get airborne from short runways, giving it added power to assist the two turboprop engines.)

We taxied to the extreme end of the runway, and as the temperature had increased dramatically, we wanted all the runway we could get. As we sat there checking things, I noticed a lot of artillery guys taking pictures and starting to line the runway to watch our departure. We got clearance and applied the brakes and brought up the power levers but did not release the brakes; the plane started to let us know that it wanted to go, and Mr. Williams released the brakes. We started to roll down the runway, slowly picking up speed, when I looked in front of us at the end of the runway, where a bunch of guys in a deuce and a half had parked to watch us take off. They, however, were parked in the exact location that we needed at the end of the runway. We called the command tent to tell them to tell the guys to move the truck. At the same time, I leaned forward as far as I could up to the windscreen and waved my arms in a crossways manner, pointing to the side of the runway. Someone got the idea to move as we barreled directly at them; we would have broadsided them if they hadn't moved at the last second. As it was, we went off the end of the runway with the gear still down; fortunately for us, the fire support base was built on the top of a mountain, and the side of the mountain fell sharply away, giving us an additional one thousand feet of altitude, along with time to put the gear up and increase our airspeed. We put the nose down and felt the plane getting stronger, gaining altitude until we were flying properly with sufficient airspeed.

Everyone on the base thought we had crashed because we went out of sight after the end of the runway. We received a panicked call from the base asking about our condition, and we responded that next time we would like a little longer runway. We made a dash for Camp Evans and were met at the end of the runway by the commanding general's staff, who took our envelope and quickly disappeared. We took off with no particular problems, although we again used much more runway than a Mohawk typically needs. When we landed at Phu Bai, we wrote up the problems with the airplane in the logbook and hoped that some mechanical guys would be able to inject some more oomph into its performance. I don't know whether that happened, as I never flew in that ship again.

Late in the summer Mr. Williams and I were on an infrared mission and noticed tracers being fired at each other across a small river. We circled around, trying to contact the troops who were involved in the firefight, but couldn't get a response. We didn't know which side of the river our guys were on, so we couldn't ask for artillery support. Then suddenly tracers from one side of the river were directed at us. Now we knew who was friend versus foe and adjusted artillery fire accordingly.

We left the area and encountered nasty weather that was part of a frontal system bringing in thunderstorms, torrential rain and damaging winds. We tried to get into our next infrared target area and experienced turbulence so severe that we had to pull our seatbelts even tighter than they were. The plane was bouncing around so much that I couldn't reach the on/off controls for the infrared system, and even if I could, the imagery would have been unusable because of the turbulence. I finally had to grab the top left corner of the infrared controls to be able to reach the toggle to turn off the system.

We couldn't get into any of our remaining target areas and couldn't land at our home base because of the weather. We had one option open us, and that was to fly south, land at a large Air Force base and spend the night at the pilots' officers' club. That is exactly what we did until dawn, when the weather cleared enough for us to take off and head home. That weather front was the forewarning of Typhoon Bess, which arrived a few days later with wind and rain that did all it could to blow our tents away and drown us, but we staked the tents securely and tried our best not to drown. We even parked our deuce and a half upwind and close to our most exposed tents to try to add some protection from the typhoon.

Mr. Williams, our lone warrant officer, was looking for something to do, as he had maxed out his flying hours and had to find something else to occupy his free time until he could fly again. At the extreme end of our platoon area was some open space that cried out to be turned into a basketball court. The only problem was that it needed to be slightly graded because it was wet—not standing water, but rather a lower area where rain water would settle until it evaporated or disappeared. Mr. Williams used his persuasive personality to borrow a D-9 Caterpillar tractor (which he said he knew how to operate) to grade the future basketball area in preparation for putting down a hard surface. When he arrived at our platoon area driving the D-9, we cheered him on, as he looked like he knew what he was doing. He swung the D-9 around, lowered the blade and started to grade the area. Everything was going well until he got too much wet muck in the blade, at which point the D-9 started to go down like it had found quicksand. Mr. Williams tried valiantly to extricate the tractor from an increasingly dire situation. We stood silently for a moment before offering him directions, instructions and other useless suggestions as he tried to reverse the D-9 out of the mire. He raised the blade, and the treads dug themselves deeper and deeper into the quagmire as he tried to back out of the muck. Finally defeated, he jumped down from the seat, and we had to throw him a rope to pull him out of the muck. (As a side note, it probably took a week of him standing outside in the rain with a bar of soap to get the stench of the mud off him.) The D-9 was hopelessly trapped, and our intrepid warrant officer had to summon help to unstick it. Later that day, another, larger Caterpillar tractor arrived with thick chains that were attached to the stuck D-9, and with patience and lots of luck and skill, the professional driver was able to pull the tractor out of the muck. Needless to say, we did not get our basketball court.

On a slight hill next to our platoon area, across rolls of concertina wire, was a Marine Corps in-country club. Marines would be sent to that club for a couple of days to drink, play cards, listen to music and harass us. Many nights we would be sitting in our tents writing or getting ready for a nighttime mission when we would hear the noise of a canister being opened. Sometimes it was just a smoke grenade that the Marines would pop and toss into our area, but other times we would hear the pop and someone would yell, "Gas!" and we would scramble to put on our gas masks as a CS grenade fell into our midst. We could hear the Marines laughing as they watched us in the dark running around trying to get upwind of the fumes. Our CO didn't think it was funny either, and the next day he went to the Marine club and reamed out the club commanding officer. All was quiet vis-à-vis smoke grenades and CS grenades for about two weeks; then the harassment started again. This time, however, we were ready, and two or three of our maintenance guys were able to get close enough to the Marine club's rear trash door to toss CS grenades into the club from the rear. Marines erupted from windows, doors and any other opening that could be found. The next day, a Marine officer visited with our CO, and a formal truce was established.

All four of our pilots were very good at their profession and proved it time and time again with their flying skills and the confidence they had with the airplanes. I had many experiences that could have turned out very unpleasant if not for the skill of the pilots. We also had a lot of fun with the airplanes, doing hours of treetop flying, buzzing fire support bases and, on a few occasions, having mock dog fights with other Mohawks. These dog fights were spur-of-the-moment affairs, as we never flew with another ship; rather, the dog fights would happen if we came across a Mohawk from another unit. Then the fun began, as each of us tried to get on the other plane's tail. These dog fights didn't last very long—just long enough to gain bragging rights before each of us continued on to our mission areas.

Sometimes our daylight missions became somewhat boring, especially if we didn't find anything worth investigating, so we would spice things up a little by testing some of the capabilities of the airplane. Diving into a river valley and roaring upriver, ruffling the surface of the water, always brought grins from both of us. It was even more fun if we found a sampan that probably contained supplies for the VC (even if we couldn't prove it). We were not going to waste a fire mission on a single sampan, so we would buzz the boat, and because our drop tanks looked exactly like bombs, the occupants of the boat who saw us coming would think that we were on a bombing run and abandon ship and swim for shore. These sampans did not contain innocent fishermen because we didn't notice any fishing nets or poles or other fishing-related equipment. We would report our sighting and location if anyone wanted to send a helicopter or gunboat to check out the situation. After doing our impromptu river recon, we felt that some higher-altitude aerobatics would be necessary. Gain some altitude, go into a dive, pull up and do a loop. Then go inverted to shake loose any empty Coke cans that had lodged under our seats. The crew chiefs didn't appreciate the inverted maneuver because sometimes the gyro would get unseated, or something like that, and they would have to reposition it.

Two of our pilots always wanted me and some of the other TOs, if we were interested, to learn to fly on autopilot. Since only A model Mohawks had dual flight controls and we didn't have any of those, we only had the autopilot to work with to fly the plane. The autopilot was simple: The control was on the console between us and slightly to the rear of my left elbow, and it was activated with a toggle switch with a round knob that looked like a small hockey puck with indentations around the diameter. Once the toggle switch was flipped to the "on" position, the airplane was controlled by using the hockey puck to turn left and right, and if you pushed down on the front edge, the airplane's nose would lower to lose altitude. To gain altitude, you simply pulled the front of the rotary control up or pressed down on the back portion. The autopilot allowed the pilot to release the control stick and relax because the plane would fly straight and level as the hockey puck, when released, would return to a neutral position.

Many times Major Taylor would look at me and say, "You've got it; turn on the autopilot," and I would hit the toggle switch and take control of the airplane. One time when I was told to take control, I forgot or didn't pull the toggle switch enough to turn on the autopilot and was puzzled that the plane responded exceedingly slowly to my hockey puck commands. Finally, I looked back and down and discovered that the autopilot was not engaged. I looked at the major and said, "I forgot to hit the toggle switch to turn the autopilot on; it's on now." He looked at me and said, "I know—now take us home."

During one uneventful mission, the major and I talked about what would happen if he became injured and couldn't fly the airplane. A large part of the discussion was the possibility of landing the plane using only the autopilot. I did have access to the landing gear lever, the flaps and the power and prop controls, but no pedals for braking and turning. An additional problem was that the autopilot would shut off at 72 knots, leaving me with no control for the airplane. We discussed and evaluated several scenarios, including an unconscious pilot with an undamaged airplane and what possible survival options could be employed (for example, trying to land the plane on autopilot while knowing the limitations of that method). That scenario would unfold as follows: I would declare an emergency and, if possible, have another Mohawk get into the air and fly alongside me to advise when to slow the plane, when to start to lower the flaps, when to start to descend and properly align with the runway, and finally lower the gear. This second airplane, if available, would escort mine all the way to the ground, pulling up at the last minute. With all of that accomplished, I would continue to decrease airspeed and altitude and make final alignment adjustments. Because I had no steering or braking controls, the only thing I could do as soon as the plane touched the runway would be to pull back on the power and prop levers, disarm both ejection seats and hang on as the plane took its own course on the ground. There was no way that I could reverse the propellers without having some directional control. The best that we could hope for under those circumstances was that the plane would simply run off the runway into the grass or sand and then stop.

The other scenario involved a plan to eject from the plane when the pilot could not do it himself. The ejection seat could be deployed via a loop directly above your head (which you would pull out and down, triggering the seat) or a handle on the seat front between your legs (which would trigger the seat when you pulled up on it). The problem arose if the pilot could not trigger the seat himself by not being able to use either ejection option. No TO I knew of would ever consider punching out and leaving the pilot injured or unconscious in the cockpit. We had to design a plan that would allow the TO to safely activate the pilot's seat. You simply couldn't reach across and pull down on top loop because, before you could move your arm back, the seat would trigger and your arm would eject with the pilot. Likewise, you couldn't easily reach the handle on the front bottom of the seat without losing your hand or arm when the seat went off. One of the best ideas that we thought about was using a boot lace that was tied to the top loop and pulled forward and down to the stick and around it back to the TO, who could then pull hard on the lace, which would pull the loop, triggering the seat. The TO could then eject. Thankfully, we never had to attempt any of the scenarios I described. I don't know whether anyone from the Army or Grumman ever landed a Mohawk on autopilot, but I assume it can be done if you have a long, wide runway and no crosswind with wide grassy areas on both sides of the runway.

Major Taylor and I were approaching Phu Bai for landing at the end of a photo/VR mission when we were advised of very strong crosswinds coming from the ocean. As we came closer to the field, we heard the tower tell a plane on short final to go around. The winds were gusting so strongly that it made landing a dangerous endeavor. We listened as a second arriving plane on short final was told to go around, and both planes were instructed to divert to another field. We continued to approach the runway and advised the tower that we were going to attempt to land. They again advised us of the gusting crosswinds but did not tell us to divert. The major said to me, "We are going to land because we do not have enough fuel to divert to another field except for a fire support base, and I really do not want to go there." He went on to say, "Sometimes in certain conditions, you have to fly the plane onto the runway and not let it float down like we normally do." *Float down*—I had never been in a Mohawk that floated down onto a runway, but I had flown with the major for so many hours for the past few months that anything he said about flying was the absolute truth.

The tower cleared us for landing, and I could see them looking out the window at our approach, being buffeted by the winds, but we came on, undeterred. The major kept our speed up, way above our normal landing speed, and lined us up for the runway. The plane bucked and jumped, but the major never flinched, concentrating on the numbers and the center of the runway. We came in low and fast, and as we went over the numbers, he flew the plane onto the runway. In quick sequence, he pulled the power levers back, applied the brakes and reversed the propellers. We used more runway than normal, but still had plenty left, and exited onto the taxiway. The tower immediately hailed us with a great landing acclamation, and they cleared us to our parking area. I looked at the major as I said, "Cold and unlocked"; he acknowledged the same as I said, "That was a fantastic learning experience and not a bad landing either." He looked at me and grinned.

Another time Major Taylor and I were on an infrared mission near the DMZ and slightly to the west. We were running the system along the side of a ridge where our intelligence had reported suspected activity. Our job was to run along the side of the ridge and look for hot spots or anything else that looked out of place. The infrared system was operating fine, and I could easily pick out trails that wove in and out of the

Nose to nose with a Mohawk (note the nose camera window).

The shrapnel piece that bounced off my head.

vegetation. The ease of seeing the trails with the equipment indicated that they were frequently used and in good condition. I pointed these out to the major while I consulted my map, which did not indicate any trails—only jungle. This was a good find, as it proved the intelligence was accurate. The trails were not visible during the daytime, but the infrared had no problem showing them because of the heat differentiation between the jungle and the hard surface of the trails. We radioed our findings back to Camp Evans, which wanted to look at the infrared film as soon as it was developed in the morning.

I went back to looking at my system after our communication with headquarters and started to see minute hot spots that were off the trails. As I looked more closely at one of the trails, it disappeared. At the point where the trail vanished, I detected a hot spot. "Hmmm," I wondered as I pointed out the location on the system and on my map to the major. "I wonder if we have found a tunnel entrance with a fire inside?" I had marked the location and coordinates on my map, and the major said, "Let's see if we can find evidence of any other possible tunnel entrances." We flew along that ridge side, and my system indicated the locations of other possible tunnel entrances. Most of these suspicious locations on the ridge showed as cold spots on the infrared terrain display indicator screens, indicating to me that these were tunnel entrances that did not have fires inside them but showed as cold because the tunnel entrances were colder at night than the surrounding jungle and trail. We asked for a fire mission and stood away as the ridge side was blasted by artillery shells. We advised the artillery people that the targets were most likely caves and that we could not give a bomb damage assessment. That assessment would have to wait until morning, when a company of 1st Cavalry grunts could be inserted. The fire mission continued for about ten minutes, covering the coordinates we had given them. They asked whether we had noticed any secondary explosions, and we responded that we had not. We left the area; because of the bombardment, our infrared equipment would be useless.

The next morning we returned to the ridge side area and monitored the grunts on the ground, who confirmed that we had indeed discovered

Sometimes the ground fire does not miss—they even got the Cavalry patch.

Me, in the cockpit TO seat, checking my infrared equipment. Note the ejection seat loop behind my head.

a large tunnel complex used as a supply depot during the Tet offensive. This depot was important because of its relative proximity to the city of Hue. A couple of days later, when we were receiving our mission briefing for the night, we noticed an alert about a "heavy artillery" (B-52) strike that night and were told to avoid that area. The coordinates were for the supply depot ridge side that we had discovered. A B-52 strike on that area would ensure that the tunnels and supply depot would be destroyed.

7

Dad, Can I Use the
Family Car?

"Dad" in this case was Major Taylor; the family car was his assigned jeep. Whenever I asked to use the "family car," I was never refused, because out of all those who used it, I was the only one who brought it back with a full tank of gas. There was nowhere to go in Phu Bai, as we were not allowed in the village and didn't want to go there anyway. I used the jeep to go to the mess hall and to the outskirts of the green line perimeter to practice shooting with my .38 and a borrowed M-16. I would always bring two or three boxes of ammunition for the .38 and two bandoliers of M-16 ammo. Each bandolier held ten 20-round magazines. I would drive to the green line, go through a gate in the wire and proceed about half a mile to a small valley or ravine. The top of the gully was only thirty or forty feet wide, with a flat field across from me that extended several hundred yards to the edge of the jungle.

I would bring several empty Coke cans with me and set them up at varying distances across the gully. The closest target was thirty or forty feet from me, which I used for practice with my .38. I would load six rounds and fire them as fast as I could to see how accurate I could be. I usually shot a box of fifty rounds and became very accurate with the revolver. I would use the M-16 for targets that ranged from fifty to two hundred feet away from me across the gully. I would fire a combination of full auto bursts and single shots. The full auto was interesting because you could only do three quick trigger pulls before the entire 20-round magazine was empty. I would use all the ammunition in one bandolier and keep the second for a just-in-case situation. I would typically throw an empty Coke can across the ravine and let it start to roll back down the hill before I started shooting at it. The intent was to continuously hit the can and try to make it go back up the hill. It was fun doing this exercise with my .38 and then switching to the M-16 and blasting off a whole magazine. There was not much left of the can when I was accurate.

I was out there one day making a lot of noise when two Green Berets and five or six Montagnard tribesmen arrived to do some shooting. They carried a vast array of weapons, from M-16s with folding stocks to World War II weapons, French rifles, Chinese burp guns, American grease guns and M-1 carbines and several different kinds of pistols. I had a chance to fire some of those weapons and found that I was not very accurate with a couple of them—namely, the grease gun and one of the Chinese pistols. One of the Green Berets amazed me with the accuracy he displayed with my borrowed M-16, as he put it on full auto and put the entire twenty rounds from one magazine into a single hapless Coke can; there was nothing left of it except shards of metal. After they left, I realized that I needed a lot more practice if I wanted to duplicate the Green Beret's accuracy. I went there once a week to practice but never could shoot like that Green Beret. With all the noise I made, I was surprised that I never met anyone else on my private shooting range.

Now I was ready to pull guard duty. About a dozen of us were scheduled to pull guard duty on the green line perimeter. We got into our deuce and a half and proceeded to the green line, where we were split up and assigned to specific bunkers. There were three guys to each bunker, equipped with an M-60 machine gun, claymore mines, boxes of hand grenades, flares, a starlight scope, an M-79 grenade launcher with a bag of extra grenades, and our own weapons with boxes of ammunition in each bunker. We broke into one-man three-hour shifts, and mine was from midnight to 3:00 a.m. I climbed onto the roof of the bunker with the M-60 machine gun, claymore mine triggers, a radio, the M-79 and my weapons. I rearranged some sandbags to offer protection from the front and settled down behind the rooftop sandbags to keep my silhouette as low as possible in case a sniper was active.

Around 2:00 a.m., the radio crackled from a bunker three buildings to my right, advising that they saw movement to the front of them at the end of the field near the jungle. I picked up the starlight scope that I had just laid down and scanned the area in front of my bunker and to the right. I stared through the view port of the scope, trying to adjust to the greenish display, when I noticed movement. The movement was quite a ways off, just at the edge of the jungle. The movements were slow and deliberate and paused every few seconds; then they would start up again, not coming toward us but parallel to our bunker line. Four bunkers in a row called in the movement, but no one was authorized to fire. As I watched, the starlight scope gave me a clearer view and the movement turned into a tiger. Two of the other bunkers also reported the tiger. I watched the tiger for a few more seconds when he suddenly bounded back into the jungle. My excitement finally settled down, and my watch ended without any other interesting events happening, except for endless numbers of rats scampering throughout the bunker and clouds of mosquitoes attacking every part of my body.

My next guard duty experience was more disgusting than exciting. We were assigned a green line sector bunker that was on a hill overlooking an ARVN compound. The ARVNs (South Vietnamese troops) were famous for shooting all night at shadows and anything that moved (or that they thought moved). They even shot in our direction more frequently than we liked. Needless to say, we kept our heads down and were on edge all night, as the shooting was heavy at times and we didn't know what was happening. Finally, most of the shooting stopped, and a light to medium rain started to fall. It was my turn to take a break, but I was not about to climb inside that bunker; who knew what could be living or slithering around inside? I chose to get inside an empty CONEX container without a door on it to get out of the rain. Someone had placed a cot in the container, so I took advantage of that and lay down to nap, but before I had even put my head down, something jumped onto my boot, ran up my leg and onto my stomach and chest, and finally catapulted off my forehead. This was followed immediately by three more of these body runners. I jumped up swearing while wildly swinging my helmet at the acrobatic rats. This indignity was too much for me to handle, and I gladly accepted sitting in the rain on the bunker roof.

This next guard duty episode happened to another guy who lived in tent a hundred feet away from mine: All of us who lived in six tents in a row were called for guard duty. Because we all went at the same time, our tents were empty. Later that night or early morning, one of the guys got sick and was relieved of duty and brought back to our platoon area. The poor guy was suffering from headaches, stomachaches, vomiting and diarrhea, and he simply wanted to climb into his bunk. His bunk was at the back far right side of the tent, and with little light, the guy could barely make out stuff thrown on the floor and his entire area in disarray. "Whiskey, tango, foxtrot," he said out loud as he approached his area; all he wanted to do was rest, but some bastard had messed up his area and was now lying in his bunk, but with the very dim light, he couldn't tell who it was. Being in a feverish state of mind, he walked up to his bunk and kicked it as hard as he could. The response was instantaneous, as the loudest growl and roar in the universe emanated from his disheveled bunk. A tiger had discovered the enticing aroma of the contents of a care package and slipped into the tent to investigate. Since there was no one around to bother it, the tiger made itself at home, ate the contents of the care package (especially enjoying the salami and bologna), and then tore everything else apart looking for more. Our hapless trooper evidently ate in bed, and the tiger investigated that too, knocking down the mosquito netting and partially destroying the bunk. After the bunk kicking and roaring noises, both parties hastily departed in opposite directions. Our trooper forgot about being sick, and the tiger disappeared out of our platoon area and through the green line back into the jungle.

Snakes were everywhere, and one of our guys found a relatively small one near our shower. He was a southern boy and very confident around snakes, as he later told us that he had captured water moccasins, copperheads and all kinds of other snakes. Some he kept as pets for a while, and the others he either killed or released back into the wild. The poisonous ones were killed so that no members of his family would be bitten. This snake he found was minding its own business but was very close to entering our washroom/shower shack. Our brave trooper thought that he should intervene so that no one—the snake or one of our guys—would get hurt. As he approached the snake to capture it barehanded, our first sergeant approached and nearly had a coronary, as he immediately identified the snake as a viper—an extremely dangerous and deadly viper. You know, the three-stepper variety, which means, after you are bitten, you can take three steps before you die. There is not a known antidote, nor would there be time even if one existed. Sarge screamed at the guy not to touch the snake and to move away as cautiously as possible. Our southern gentleman did as he was told, and the sergeant clobbered the snake with an entrenching tool. He then told all of us who had gathered around to watch the events to look closely at the snake, remember what it looked like and never approach one.

When we could, we would drive to the other unit's mess hall for midnight chow. We were glad that it was dark, so that we could not see what we were trying to eat. Usually, just to be safe, we would each have a fried egg sandwich on white bread with ketchup; at least you could identify what you had on your plate. In the morning, after flying all night, we would usually arrive just after the mess hall shut down for the morning. There were no exceptions to the operating hours, as the head chef (i.e., mess sergeant) would loudly exclaim, "I don't care what you have been doing; it's not my responsibility to keep this mess hall open all day just for you—it is up to you to get here while we are open." Therefore, after flying all night, we were not going to be fed again. We probably would miss lunch too, as we were trying to get some rest in our tents, and with the intense heat and humidity, a restful sleep was difficult to achieve. Much of the time, I had just gotten to sleep and did not want to fully awaken to walk two miles to the mess hall just to have some kind of mystery meat and powdered junk for lunch. When I did finally fully awaken, I would grab a box of C-rations and hope for the best—maybe some pears in a thick sauce, or miniature hot dogs in something that was somewhat edible. Have you ever seen tropical chocolate bars or tried to eat one? All you need is a hammer or rock to break off a chunk and possess a stomach that is stupid enough to try to digest that stuff.

We lived for the moment a care package arrived from home that was full of homemade cookies, hard salami, instant soup and anything else that would survive the heat and humidity during such a long journey. Hershey's chocolate bars did not do well on their journey, melting so badly that they made a chocolatey mess out of everything else in the box. Sharp or extra sharp cheddar cheese fared a little better; it did melt somewhat, but at least it did not become cheese soup. C-rations were interesting, as we undoubtedly had cases left over from World War II or at least from Korea (or so it seemed when you opened a case). We had an interesting invention called a P-38 can opener—it was small, flat and less than two inches long, with a blade that would swing out from the small handle. You would hook it onto the side of the tip lid and rotate the blade to cut into the top of the can while you rotated the opener around the upper edge. Some of the cans of food were pretty good, and some were only good to feed to swine. You were certainly lucky to open a can of pear halves in syrup. I still have a P-38 today.

MREs had not been invented yet, or if they were, we never saw them. We just hoped for the best when we opened a box of C-rations.

8

Tents versus Hooches

My tour in Vietnam can be divided into two sections: The first was six months of living in an eight- or ten-man tent that was full of shrapnel holes, infested with rats and bloody hot, as the Aussies put it. During the second six months, I lived in a wooden hooch that had screen and board walls and a roof. The hooch was large enough to be divided into 8 foot × 10 foot rooms with floor-to-ceiling walls and a door. There were four rooms on each side of the hooch, with a center aisle connecting the front door to the rear door. The hooches with the screen and board walls were built with wide spaces between the boards to allow airflow to go through the entire structure, and the screens kept the bugs out. Tents, by contrast, did not have screens and were heat sinks, keeping the heat and humidity trapped inside the tent.

The monsoon season arrived, trapping us in our leaking tents. We had to roll down the sides to keep some of the sideways-blowing rain from soaking everything in the tents. It didn't rain—it poured heavily day and night, endlessly, for twenty-eight days. Nothing was dry any longer, as you became soaked to the skin as soon as you left the tent. Even wearing a poncho didn't help because the wind blew the poncho around so much that you stopped wearing one and simply got soaked. Sleeping at night was a problem because the monsoon brought a drop in temperature; our sleeping bags were a welcome addition to our bunks— that is, until they, too, became so damp that you didn't want to use one. There was no way to dry them out enough to be comfortable. I would hang mine inside my tent over some empty ammo boxes, but the wind and rain and humidity would keep the bag damp at best. My poncho liner fared a little better and kept me fairly comfortable at night. All of my clothing was either very wet or very damp. Any time you ventured out of the tent to go to the mess hall, you rode in the back of a truck, and that was the name of the game: wet, cold, hungry and miserable.

I was down to my last pair of slightly damp socks when our first sergeant called everyone together in the rain. We were needed to shovel a passageway for the water that had inundated three tents that were in a slight depression just above our tents. The water had risen so deeply inside the tents that guys lying on air mattresses on their bunks were washed outside. We had to dig a channel across—essentially a sandbar— to allow the water to drain away. We made a trench about two and a half feet deep and ten feet long to allow the water to drain away from the low area that had flooded the tents.

We of course could not fly in those conditions, and even if we could, the photos (both camera and infrared) would be worthless. We nearly went out of our minds with boredom while dealing with the continuing wetness and cold. The only thing we could do was go to our club, drink and play card games. I played one hand of poker, promptly lost ten dollars that I could not afford to lose, and sat in a corner to find something to read. Several guys were really into their poker games, and losing a month's pay was not uncommon.

9

Midnight Requisitions Courtesy of the United States Marine Corps

As I have previously stated, our first sergeant was a wheeler/dealer extraordinaire—the king and undisputed champion of the outhouse transaction. He announced to us one day that we needed a new shower shack. Truer words were never spoken, as our current shower shack was just that: a shack that was dangerous beyond words, one you used only when you couldn't stand yourself any longer. It was rickety with a rotten floor that let any and all rats in to watch us shower—the sneaky little perverts. The ceiling was falling in due to the weight of a 55-gallon drum that was on the roof and contained our shower water, which we filled every day. If you wanted a shower with warm or hot water, you showered at midday. If you wanted a cool shower, you went at night or first thing in the morning. The shower held only one person at a time, and you had to be careful not to back into a wall, as it was likely to fall over or onto you. We definitely needed a new shower shack.

The first sergeant, as usual, had the answer: "We will visit the Marine Corps supply depot tonight and see what they have in stock." He had learned through years of dealing with the Army's red-tape system for requesting supplies that we would have better luck asking for a full restroom (I mean latrine) with flush toilets, hot and cold running water and electricity. As promised, the sergeant asked for volunteers to accompany him on a "fact-finding outing" that night around midnight or later. Six or seven of us thought that was a wonderful idea and committed to the plan. Around midnight, we climbed into our deuce and a half truck and drove to the other end of the airfield to another company's mess hall (that was where we normally ate) for midnight chow. Every unit had people working around the clock, so midnight was a normal time to eat. After an interesting tray full of unidentifiable slop, we climbed back into our truck and headed for the United States Marine Corps supply depot located next to the airfield in Phu Bai.

The supply depot was not illuminated, to keep mortars and rockets from pinpointing its location, and it was rather large, covering a quarter-mile square, with a tall chain-link fence and rolls of concertina wire at the base of the fence. We approached the entrance of the depot, and a Marine Corps private hailed us. The sergeant, who was driving, told the sentry that we needed to do a quick inventory of their supplies to be sure that items we needed were available to requisition in the morning. The poor Marine looked a little puzzled at first, as he was trying to understand why seven Army guys in a big Army truck would want to look at supplies in a Marine Corps depot. Sarge told him that we did it all the time and it was a new interservice cooperative effort. He said all that as he passed a pint of liquor to the sentry, who looked at the pint like it was his new best friend. Being very careful not to drop his new treasure, the sentry unlocked the gate for us and motioned us through.

Sarge told us to be quick, as the Marine duty officer would probably come by soon, and he would not be as understanding as the private. Sarge had told us at midnight chow what we needed to look for. Soon lumber of all sorts, plywood, two by fours, bags of cement, hammers, saws, nails and many other sundry items found their way onto our truck.

One of the other guys said, "Sarge, look what I found." It was an icemaker—boy, could we use an icemaker! The sergeant looked at it and said, "Our generator does not have enough oomph to power that as well as the other critical things that need electric power in our platoon area, so you know what that means." We were all crestfallen. Then he said, "You know what that means—it means that we have to find a heavy-duty generator to go with our new icemaker." We quickly searched and found just what we were looking for. It joined the icemaker in the truck as we looked around for the Marine duty officer.

Sarge quietly told us to get aboard and drove toward the gate, where the sentry was still guarding his pint but moved to unlock the gate to let us out. As we drove away, we turned on our blackout lights and headed back to our platoon area. While driving, we noticed a jeep approaching us with two Marines in it. We were a significant distance from the depot and couldn't tell whether the jeep contained the duty officer, as the depot entrance was out of sight. We soon returned to our platoon area, and everyone went to their tents.

In the morning, around 6:00, I was walking to the flight line for a mission when I heard a slight crunch. I turned in time to see the sergeant behind the wheel of our deuce and a half as he "accidently" backed over our old shower shack, reducing it to splinters. Later that afternoon, when I had finished my recon mission, I was surprised to see a brand new shower shack that was almost operational (we had to let our new cement floor dry before we could use it). I also heard a new powerful noise and looked toward our club and saw a new generator pumping out voltage that was converted into ice cubes. Sometimes you do what you have to do to make a miserable situation somewhat less miserable!

10

He Said That He Would
Not Be Going Home

He just showed up one day in midsummer 1968, a slightly over-weight, grungy-looking guy with filthy fatigues, unshaven with a different look in his eye. You could tell that he was not new to Vietnam; he looked like he had been in-country for quite a while. Our company clerk only knew that the guy had radio experience, and since our airplanes contained several radios, someone somewhere decided that he should be sent to us to assist with our radios. The guy kept to himself (which was probably OK, as his hygiene was atrocious) and didn't try to interact with anyone. This was a bit strange, as we only numbered about thirty people, but we respected his privacy.

About two weeks after the guy arrived, I found him in the early evening in our club having a beer. (Our club was a tent with a small counter and a beer and Coke cooler filled with ice.) I had just come down from flying all day and needed something cold, either a beer or a Coke (or several of both).

Before I continue, I have to tell you about our beer. It consisted of one brand, and that was Carling Black Label in *rusty* steel cans. The cases of Carling had evidently been sent via ship and spent the entire voyage in the bottom of the ship submerged in sea water—hence the rust. You had to be careful how you handled them, as they could crush if you held them too tightly, leaving you with a handful of rust. The beer tasted awful! (The Aussies had huge cans of fresh Foster's brand beer that was incredible, but that is another story to be shared later.)

Our club had a few folding chairs, and as I sat down with my can of Coke, the strange new guy looked up and said hello. He had been in the club most of the afternoon, and the pile of empty beer cans were testament to that. He had changed to hard liquor and had trouble staying in his chair, as he was swaying like a ship in a storm. He asked whether I had been flying; I responded that I had been flying photo recon missions all day to the west. I mentioned a couple of fire support bases, and he, to my surprise, said, "Hey, I know that area real well." I asked him how he knew the area, and he took a moment or two to reply: "I was a radio man, a grunt who carried a PRC-25 radio on my back for our platoon leader. I did that until the two of us got shot; the lieutenant was killed, and I was slightly wounded, but not bad enough to keep me out of the field for long." He continued, "Not long after that, we visited a fairly secure village or town, and I visited some of the local ladies; they unfortunately were not the ones that had mandatory physicals, and I caught something from them." He went to see a medic friend of his, who immediately took him to an Army hospital. He said, "The doctors gave me penicillin and other antibiotics that seemed to work at first, but then I got sicker and sicker. I became a liability and was sent to several different outfits and saw several different doctors, each giving me different treatments but with the same results." He looked at me and said, "That is how I ended up with you guys. I expect to be here a short time; they told me that I cannot go home in this condition but they would continue to try to help me; they can't even send me to Japan until they can identify my disease."

He then got to his feet, and as he was about to leave, he looked at me and said, "This information is between you and me, UNDERSTAND!" I sat there thinking, "Holy crap, this guy is stuck in Vietnam forever or until a cure can be found for his problem." He had told me his name— John—but no other personal information. I kept his story to myself, as he requested, but wondered whether he had told anyone else about his situation.

About a week later, in the middle of a dark night, one of our Mohawks landed with a warning light illuminated. The pilot kept both engines running to allow the crew chief, who had opened access doors on the side of the fuselage, to test some of the sending units to identify the fault. The crew chief had his head inside the fuselage and didn't notice John come up from behind the airplane, pass under the wing and walk directly into the spinning propeller. There was a loud pop when the first of three propeller blades hit him. The pilot looked down at the noise, as it was the propeller on his side of the airplane that John had walked into. He quickly shut down the engines as he called on the radio for medics. There was nothing anyone could do except bring a body bag.

John was finally going home.

11

The Marines and the Boomerang Does Come Back

Summer, Phu Bai, Vietnam. One of our platoon members had just returned from his R&R in Australia and brought several boomerangs back with him. Two or three were beautifully hand carved and quite large, at least two or more feet long. These were serious boomerangs. He also had three smaller boomerangs that were designed to teach you how to properly throw a boomerang. Several of us went to an open area outside of our platoon area to practice throwing these boomerangs so that they would come back to us. We learned quickly—quicker than we thought—and began to throw these boomerangs fairly accurately, with them returning to the thrower and spinning in the air over his head. The secret to capturing your thrown boomerang was to watch it spinning over your head and quickly stick your hand in the circle made by the spinning boomerang and grab it. That technique worked almost every time—either that, or we throwers were very lucky not to lose any fingers.

We never tried to hit anything with those boomerangs; there was nothing living out in that beach sand that was even slightly edible. There were Marines, though, but we were told to never molest dumb, innocent animals, so we ignored them until....

Just across some concertina wire in the open area very near us, a squad or two of Marines were marched in by a sergeant. These Marines had evidently done something that displeased their sergeant, and he was getting them ready to do physical training in this hot, sandy, dusty open field as punishment. As they marched in formation, they watched us throwing our boomerangs and were impressed with our ability to make them come back to the throwers. One of our guys thought it would be fun to throw a boomerang toward the Marines and make it return in a low-level pass, just over their heads. It worked perfectly until the boomerang failed to gain enough altitude to clear the concertina wire. It just barely caught the top strand of wire and bounced back toward the Marines.

We yelled to the Marine sergeant and asked him if he could please return our boomerang to us. Instead of simply tossing it across the wire (which was a distance of five feet), he hauled back and threw that boomerang as hard as he could at us. The boomerang took the hint and immediately headed directly for us; then it gracefully gained altitude, went into a beautiful slow climbing turn to the left and headed almost out of sight—almost. The boomerang continued on its banking flight as the Marine sergeant went about his business, completely ignoring the flight of the boomerang. The boomerang then dutifully turned to its thrower. The sergeant was now completely engrossed in deciding which physical exercises his Marines should attempt first. Meanwhile, all of us and many of the Marines were watching the path of the incoming boomerang as it homed in on its thrower. Several Marines ducked as the boomerang hit the sergeant in the middle of his upper back.

Incensed, the sergeant picked up the boomerang and threw it as hard as he could at us. Again, the boomerang, taking a clue from its previous flight, took off as though it was going back to Australia, but, halfway there, it remembered that it was supposed to return to the person who threw it. This time the boomerang's timing was perfect, as it caught the sergeant in the back of his head, just as he was giving a tirade to his troops. Fortunately, this boomerang was a practice one, not one used for hunting, which could have given the sergeant a nasty injury. (I can hear his explanation while getting his head stitched up: "The VC have perfected the use of attack boomerangs.")

All of us ran to the wire and asked if he was OK, but, being the staunch Marine that he was, the sergeant simply swore and picked up the boomerang. Before he could cause more injury by throwing the boomerang again, one of our guys reached through the concertina wire and said, "Sarge, just hand it to me before you hurt anyone else." This really pissed him off, and we were thankful that the wire was between us, as this Marine was huge! Fortunately, one of his Marines stepped up and took the boomerang from him and tossed it to us.

I forgot to mention that after the boomerang hit the sergeant in the head, all of his Marines and all of us laughed so hard that we fell onto the sand; we all looked like we were having seizures. This laughter coming from his Marines and a bunch of Army guys was almost too much for him to handle, but his anger and humiliation were diminished when the other Marine took the boomerang from him and gave it to us.

We quickly left the area and the Marines marched back to their compound, many still snickering. We had more sessions until those practice boomerangs finally had enough and disintegrated before they could injure any more Marines.

12

The Royal Australian Air Force

The Aussies had a contingent of Royal Australian Air Force guys (mates) who lived across the runway from us at the end of the field. They flew Caribou transportation airplanes, and it was always fun to watch their planes land. We almost always had a crosswind blowing from the ocean across the runway, and every plane that landed at Phu Bai had to crab sideways to land. As the pilots turned toward the runway on their final approach, we could clearly see the nose of the plane turned slightly toward the ocean while the rest of the plane flew sideways toward the runway. The coolest thing, though, was watching the Aussie pilots with their side cockpit windows slid rearward to the fully open position, with their elbows out the window as if they were cruising in a Falcon or Holden car at home in Sydney on a Saturday night. The plane would continue sideways over the runway until, finally, the left main landing gear would make contact with the runway, and the plane would pivot to the right and the right main gear would touch down; then the nose gear would come into contact with the runway, and brakes and reverse propellers would slow the plane until it reached the taxiway. The Aussie pilots would do this maneuver each time they landed, and we never got tired of watching this display of airmanship.

The Aussies were great at trading with us for clothing, boots, hats and other souvenirs. The only problem was that we had very few goods to trade. I had been given five or six one-piece flight suits from the guys who had gone home when I arrived, but they were generally too large for my 115-pound body and unbearably hot (I think they were made for use in Germany in the winter). We could only get our hands on extra jungle boots and a few poncho liners. A group of us walked across the runway with our trade goods and met a group of Aussies who had fantastic items to trade. I received a pair of kangaroo-skin Army boots (I still have them), a boonies hat (which I still have) and a campaign slouch hat (the kind that has the side brim turned up; unfortunately, I don't have that one any longer, as, thanks to overtime and multiple relocations, the hat got eaten by mice and moths and finally had to be recycled).

My slouch hat acquired in a trade with the Royal Australian Air Force guys.

The Aussies loved the one-piece flight suits and the nylon poncho liners, which we used as blankets when needed. The liners were lightweight, camouflaged and breathable, and the Aussies were glad to trade for them. (They made great beach blankets for use on Bondi Beach.) The kangaroo-skin boots I received in exchange are soft and comfortable. The only problem I had was when the Aussie I was trading with asked me what size boot I needed. He said, "You look like you take a 43 or 44." I said, "What are you talking about? You mates have very big feet if you wear a size 43 or 44 boot; I wear a 10." We both looked at each other; then he said, "Hold up your foot and I will compare your boot to mine." I held up my foot, and he determined that I needed a slightly smaller boot than his, which meant a size 43. He returned a couple of minutes later with a brand new pair of size 43 Royal Australian Air Force or Army boots. They fit perfectly.

We continued to trade with them, but it soon became increasingly difficult, as we ran out of things to trade that anyone would be interested in having. We even tried trading our rusty cans of Carling Black Label beer to them for some of their Foster's brand beer, but they laughed at us, saying, "Isn't Vietnam bad enough for you mates without being tortured further with this cat's piss for beer?" Then they felt sorry for us and gave us a few cans of fantastic fresh, cold Foster's beer. Aussies are truly fantastic human beings!

We met another group of Aussies several months later when the 1st Cavalry Division moved south, but those Aussies were grunts, not Air Force, and were crazy-crazy good (that story to follow in Chapter 18).

13

Moonlight, B-52s and Battleship

I flew most of my missions with Major Taylor or Captain Johnson. Then we received a replacement pilot to keep our allotment to four. He was a young warrant officer, which was unusual, as most warrant officers flew helicopters, not fixed-wing aircraft. I was assigned to fly with him to assist him in learning the geography of our area.

One night about a month later, Mr. Williams and I were flying an infrared mission. The moon was full and looked huge, but the night air was putrid and so humid that we almost had trouble breathing. Our Mohawks were not equipped with air conditioning, but they did have an adjustable vent in front of the pilot and another in front of the TO. You could adjust the airflow amount and the direction by turning and swiveling the vent opening. It didn't help very much, but at least you could have some hot air directed at your face. We had finished our second target area and decided to enjoy some cooler air at a higher altitude, as the air temperature and humidity level at 800–1,000 feet were unbearable and the odor from the village below us was permeating the cockpit and nearly making us gag and gasp for fresh air.

As we gained altitude and moved away from the village, the air became increasingly fresh and cool. The full moon beckoned us to come closer, and the large snow-white clouds around us invited us to fly between them and follow the clear air canyons that led to even cooler fresh air. The air was calm as we dove and climbed from cloud to cloud. It was impossible to believe while we were up here that all that chaos was going on just a few thousand feet below us. The peacefulness and serenity were all encompassing, letting us relax for the first time in a very long time. It was so refreshing that we almost lost track of time until we looked at the fuel gauge and realized that it was time to go and return to the mayhem below us. I never experienced another full moonlit night in Vietnam in which we played among the clouds.

Reality came roaring back as we descended toward the smelly village and ran into a welcoming barrage of green and red tracers (the NVA and VC ammunition had green tracers, and captured U.S. ammo had red tracers). We banked away and called in an artillery strike at the coordinates of the incoming tracers. The guys shooting at us were not in or near the village, but they were approaching it when we arrived. The artillery responded with several volleys, and we noticed two secondary explosions. We requested that the Cavalry send in a white (scout helicopter) and red (helicopter gunship) team, followed by a blue (infantry) team in the morning to do a bomb damage assessment.

We completed our next target area and returned to our base to refuel, get bladder relief and maybe snatch some food before we took off again. We lifted off about an hour later to do a low-level visual recon in the general vicinity of the tracers to see whether we could stir up any more tracers. As it happened, we did, addressing them with another fire support mission. After the gunners finished firing their 105 howitzers, we flew around their mountaintop base. My pilot spoke with the fire support base commanding officer and asked whether the airspace around them was clear, as we wanted to surprise the artillery guys. He informed us that he did not have any fire missions and no resupply helicopters were planned. Mr. Williams looked at me and grinned, and I knew instantly what he was planning to do. We circled around the mountaintop, and I could see the artillery company guys watching us and taking pictures. We disappeared into the valley next to the fire support base and came up out of nowhere and did a low-level pass over their heads. Guys on the ground were going crazy as we gave them an airshow to remember. I can still see the guys with their cameras, snapping shot after shot as we passed about thirty feet directly above them. It made their day and gave us something to grin about.

My next mission with the new warrant officer pilot involved some hair-raising moments. We were on an IR mission and flew over our first target area with nothing to report except for a few haphazard tracer shots pointed in our general direction, but not any concentrated fire directed at us. Then we approached our next target area, which was a valley with a river in the middle of it and flat areas on both banks that ascended into low hills and then a rugged mountain range of three thousand feet on the north side of the river. Our mission was to use the IR system to map that valley for several miles in one direction over the left riverbank, turn around and run directly over the river, and turn around again and map the right riverbank (the side closer to the mountain range). We had ample moonlight left to be able to clearly see the river and the forbidding mountain range to our right. The higher ridgetops were about a mile from the river and posed no danger to us unless we did something stupid or were forced in that direction to avoid anti-aircraft fire.

As we approached the valley, we swung "feet wet" over the ocean to have a better alignment and then swung 180 degrees for our first run. While approaching the ocean end of the valley, I turned on the infrared system to map the area and did a visual recon of the river below us as the system took infrared photos of the left side of the river. As we looked out of the cockpit at the moonlit countryside, the entire riverside area below and in front of us exploded in a nightmarish fashion. The exploding debris rose up to meet us, as we were only 800 feet off the ground. My pilot immediately stood our Mohawk on its tail and just as quickly did a right wingover, and we sprinted to our left toward the ground and away from the valley.

Somehow, someone in mission planning at the division level had assigned us missions that were directly in the path of a planned "heavy artillery" (B-52) strike. We were always briefed on when and where a B-52 strike would occur so that we could avoid that general area. This time, however, we flew directly under the bombers as they delivered their payloads. I can just imagine looking out my side of the cockpit and seeing those 500-pound bombs pass by my side of the airplane mere yards away. After that experience, we both were pretty shaken up and decided to call it a night. When we landed, we were still really pissed that someone had given us a mission in the exact location of a B-52 strike and demanded an explanation. All we ever got was "mistakes happen, *sin loy*" (tough shit, live with it).

Another night mission was scheduled to be flown inland from the ocean where the topography indicated a slight rise in elevation. I was running my infrared system and started to detect small pockets of hot spots just off a small stream and trail. The hot spots were in small spread-out clusters in the jungle off the trail. I called the nearest fire support base and asked whether they had had any fire missions in that area during the day or the night before. They responded in the negative—they had not put any artillery in that area. I next asked about the possibility of any friendlies in the area and, if so, whether they had received any helicopter gunship support. The reply to both questions was negative. The evidence at hand (i.e., no artillery fire, no friendlies and no air support) led to the following conclusion: those hot spots not visible from the air could only be highly camouflaged cooking fires from an NVA company. Not just a squad or platoon, but at least a company (or an even larger force) was camped in the area based on the number and distribution of the hot spots.

We called on the net for a fire mission, but the closest fire support base was already supporting an infantry company under attack and could not assist us. Suddenly, a voice with a call sign "Volcano" (not the actual call sign but close enough) came up on the net and asked whether they could assist with a fire mission. We had no idea who they were and told them to wait; when we looked in our call-sign book, we discovered that "Volcano" was the call sign for the battleship *New Jersey*. We immediately responded in the affirmative that we indeed needed a fire support mission. The *New Jersey* was cruising several miles offshore, but its 16-inch shells could travel over twenty miles. We quickly gave them the coordinates of the hot spots (campfires) and additional information about the stream and trails so that they could see exactly on their maps where we needed the shells to impact.

In a very short amount of time, the voice came back onto our frequency and advised us to depart the area, as they were about ready to shoot. We acknowledged and advised that we were departing for an area that would allow us to watch the impact of the shells. The voice came back on, saying "Shot away," at the same time that the entire horizon on the ocean illumined like a massive volcano had just erupted. The sight is etched in my mind, as I have never since witnessed the immense wall of fire and smoke that we saw in the distance. Shortly thereafter, the ground in front of us erupted in a similar volcano effect as the nine 16-inch shells exploded along that stream and trail. The *New Jersey* had given us a full broadside, as all nine 16-inch guns were fired at the same time. The voice came back on and asked whether we needed another salvo. We replied in the negative, as all we could see was a huge wall of flames that extended up the valley near the stream. We advised that we would request a 1st Cavalry team to conduct a BDA (bomb damage assessment) in the morning and advise the *New Jersey* of the results.

A couple of days later, Mr. Williams and I were flying a daytime "feet wet" photo mission along the coast when we noticed a large ship several miles offshore that was moving at a moderate speed toward the south. We decided to investigate, and as soon as we turned toward the ship, we could tell that it was a very large warship—the *New Jersey*. A soon as we turned toward the ship, we were hailed by it and asked our intentions. We replied that we wanted to do a flyby and added that we had recently done a nighttime fire mission with the ship. They advised that we could do a flyby on their starboard side but had to stay at least a quarter mile away from the ship. We approached the *New Jersey* from the stern and slowed our speed as we flew along its starboard side. As we did that flyby, I turned the belly camera to a thirty-degree oblique to the left and turned on our camera. We took frame after frame of the ship and noticed after the film was developed that several anti-aircraft guns tracked our flight. You could see in each photo how the guns moved with us, always keeping us directly in their sights. I brought several of those photos home, but over time they have disappeared.

Flying at night was always interesting, as you never knew what to expect. The weather could change dramatically; areas that were quiet with no activity could suddenly change into a hailstorm of incoming ground fire. Other times things were quite beautiful, with the full moon illuminating the mountain ridges and valleys. Sometimes the clouds would float over the mountains, and the scenery was spectacular, with small rivers flowing out of the mountains and the fields and rice paddies forming geometric patterns in the landscape below. Many times flashes of light would illuminate the horizon, indicating either a thunderstorm or artillery activity. There was never any indication of artificial lights—only the occasional light from a small fire in a village or hamlet. We were alone up there in our own world as we flew across a mosaic of the land and watched as the dawn slowly approached from the ocean. The mountaintops, of course, received the first rays of sunlight, which made the green jungle come alive with color while the valleys remained cloaked in darkness. We would gain some altitude and admire the landscape below us. Vietnam was a truly beautiful country—at least in the I Corps area. Then it was time to return to base and face the heat and humidity until we were once again required to strap into the cockpit for the next adventure or terrifying incident.

There was always a flight that stood out because of the fun, excitement, danger, boredom or the unexpected. Periodically we would have to take a plane airborne after it was repaired for one reason or another to ascertain whether the repairs had actually fixed what was wrong. One day Captain Johnson saw me in the platoon area and asked whether I wanted to go on a maintenance check flight with him. He needed a second set of eyes on the instruments as he put the plane through some interesting maneuvers to verify that the repairs had been successful. I had been on maintenance check rides several times in the past, and each time the repairs had been completed successfully. This time, we were going to check on the function of one of the instruments to determine if the instrument had been faulty or if the sending unit was bad or if the component itself was bad. None of the above failing would have caused the plane to crash or be overly dangerous; you just wanted to have instruments performing as expected.

I have forgotten which instrument we were checking, but my job was to stare at it and confirm that it stayed in the green (or whatever it was supposed to do). If it didn't remain stable or indicate what it should, then I would tell the pilot what it was doing and we would land and tell

Mohawk belly camera photograph of another Mohawk.

the crew chief that it was still broken. The Mohawks were tough airplanes, and most of the problems arose from either an instrument malfunctioning or some type of electrical problem. Very rarely did we experience a serious malfunction that put us in danger. For example, you could have a hydraulic leak that affected the flight controls caused by ground fire or a loose fitting that was missed during the preflight inspection. Alternatively, there could be a fuel leak that led to an in-flight engine fire. We did have a fire-suppression system in the airplane that supposedly would extinguish the fire. Then we would have to fly with one engine unaffected by the fire.

This day our flight was supposed to be short because we had only one instrument to check. We got airborne and went feet wet to get away from the flight path of incoming and outgoing aircraft and increased our altitude to 10,000 feet. We wanted ample airspace to perform our instrument check, and then check it again. We went into a dive heading for the ocean, as this type of maneuver was what had initially caused the instrument to malfunction. I watched the instrument, and it was indicating whatever it was supposed to indicate correctly. I took my eyes away from the instrument and stared at the ocean coming up at us at an alarming rate of speed. At first I thought that there was something wrong with the airplane because I had confirmed to the pilot that the instrument was performing as expected and I thought that we would immediately pull up out of our dive, but we didn't pull up—we continued to dive. As I watched the ocean, I was hit with a strange calmness. I was mesmerized by the beautiful blue water, and the thought came over me that this was the day when it would end for me. I don't have any idea why I thought that way, but all I remember is this incredible calmness and acceptance of the inevitable. I didn't say anything to my pilot, but I looked at him and he, too, had a look of calmness on his face.

All this took a few seconds; then Captain Johnson gently pulled back on the stick, and the plane pulled out of its dive and settled back into a smooth horizontal flight. Neither one of us said anything, until the captain said, "Let's do a quick river recon and see if there is any activity upriver." We did an unexpected recon and didn't find anything of interest, so we headed for home, doing some exciting treetop flying. I thoroughly enjoyed the thrill of low-level flying as we zigged and zagged around trees, buzzed rice paddies and looked for anyone trying to shoot at us. Neither of us mentioned anything about what we had experienced during the dive toward the ocean, but from that day forward, I had no doubt about my surviving and going home in one piece. I certainly did have my share of close calls after that day, but I always had the feeling with me that I would not be harmed.

14

LZ in the Morning and
Jungle Clearings

Early mornings at or just before sunrise were always welcome; that meant that the nighttime mission was nearly complete and we could look forward to food, a latrine break and maybe a little rest before we climbed back into the cockpit for a daytime photo/VR mission (or two or three). Many times—actually more than many times—as the sun came up out of the ocean, we would be flying low level and approach a jungle clearing and notice faint wisps of smoke rising from the jungle at the edge of the clearing. The clearings were never very large, and perhaps one helicopter at a time could land there. The jungle surrounding these clearings was always very dense, with vegetation encroaching on all sides, which provided good cover for anyone hiding there. The morning air being rather calm, any cooking fire smoke would rise gently out of the brush and be visible for a brief time from the air.

Whenever we noticed the almost invisible smoke coming from the jungle near a clearing, we would turn to investigate the reason for the smoke. We would come in quickly at treetop level and do a visual recon of the clearing and surrounding jungle. Because the Mohawk was very quiet when approaching a target, we would be over the clearing and gone before anyone could react to our presence. On many occasions, we would see men scrambling around the edges of the clearing after hearing and seeing us zoom over them. Since we were unarmed, the only thing we could do was call the closest fire support base and request a fire mission, reporting, "Gooks in the open at coordinates xyz, we need a fire mission NOW." We would then circle out of the way and watch as the artillery shells impacted into the clearing, blowing holes in the vegetation and knocking down trees. Afterward, we would fly back and do a bomb damage assessment, both visually and with the belly camera, but we learned very quickly that the artillery strike was a waste of time, as the enemy moved out very quickly after our pass over their location.

By the time the fire mission shells impacted, the NVA troops had disappeared into the jungle to safety.

Another option we had was to make another pass over their location and mimic a bombing run to cause them to hunker down where they were while we called for the fire mission. The extra fuel tanks under our wings looked exactly like 250-pound bombs, so when we made our run, it looked like we could drop these two pseudo bombs directly into their laps. Our intent was to make the enemy take cover in or near the clearing until the fire support base could shoot a battery of rounds into the area. However, this strategy didn't work as well as we planned, because during and after our flyover, the NVA dropped what they were doing and scrambled into the safety of the jungle.

One final option we had was to get on the radio and broadcast a call for air support, reporting that we had enemy troops in the open. We hoped that the call would be answered by Air Force or Navy fast movers (jets) and they would do a bombing run. The other possibility we hoped for was to be contacted by an Army helicopter gunship flight that was escorting a quick reaction blue team of 1st Cavalry grunts that could divert to our clearing. Neither of these last two scenarios ever happened. All we could do was report the sighting and ask for a response from someone.

Another morning we spotted a company-sized force of NVA moving quickly from one small clearing to a trail along the side of a small stream. We again called for artillery support, but the NVA troops were just out of range of the 105 mm guns that the fire support base used. We did a photo run and received small-arms fire for our efforts, but, again, we were there and gone before any damage could be done to us. Treetop-level flying and the speed of the aircraft helped us avoid looking like Swiss cheese. We made another pass with the belly camera, but the NVA had disappeared into the triple canopy jungle, and we reported their last known position. We had gotten accustomed to these early morning sightings and soon realized that there was nothing we could do except report the coordinates of the sightings and continue with our mission.

One early morning, we had lifted off and were proceeding to a small river to do a photo/VR recon when we noticed a flight of helicopters ahead of and above us heading toward the same river. There were five Huey slicks carrying a platoon of 1st Cavalry troopers escorted by a pair of Huey hog gunships. They were quite a distance ahead of us and we slowed down, as we did not want to overtake them, especially since we didn't know where they were going and we did not want to get in their way. We soon found out where they were headed, as an area in front of us to the left suddenly erupted in explosions of fire and smoke as a nearby fire support base poured 105 mm howitzer shells into the LZ (landing zone) and the area around it. As we slowly approached the flight from the rear, they rapidly started to descend toward an open area on the left riverbank. The artillery fire ceased, and the slicks came in low and fast, with the Huey hogs providing cover on both sides of the flight when the gunships opened up on the LZ, firing rockets and machine-gun fire into the zone and into the jungle on each side. The gunships then fired into the LZ in front of the slicks. We held back, and the gunships went around and laid down another barrage of covering fire while the slicks touched down and the grunts leaped off helicopters and provided additional firepower to cover the Hueys as they lifted off. We stayed out of the way in case the slicks had to take evasive maneuvers to avoid the incoming ground fire.

We contacted the fire support base and received the call sign and frequency for the ground troops, and we asked each if they wanted us to do a flyby to see whether we could spot any enemy troops. They responded in the affirmative, and we circled around, went to tree-top level and blasted across the LZ with the camera taking frame after frame. We made another pass from a different direction and did not receive any ground fire. The LZ was now cold, and the grunts could relax and continue to skirmish along the riverbank, while we left to do our river recon.

We had a mountain valley visual recon assigned to us, and as we headed for the area, I could see thunderhead clouds developing, but they were far enough away to give us time to finish in our target area before they could affect us. The valley was between two ridges and served as a direct route to a river that was used for transporting supplies and troops (not ours). We wanted to see whether we could find evidence of recent use of the trails through the valley. We were warned about incoming small-arms fire, as several helicopters in recent days had been damaged (with one shot down). The valley was deep with heavy jungle vegetation, and I wondered how we would be able to see any trails. The mountain ridges had steep sides covered with thick vegetation that would offer anyone ample cover to shoot at targets in the valley or flying into it. I said to my pilot, "Here we go into the mouth of the dragon." We entered the valley and almost immediately started to receive small-arms fire that did no damage to the airplane. We completed our run and agreed that there was no way any airplane or helicopter could find trails, much less assess them for recent usage. We considered a nighttime infrared mission but dismissed that idea as unlikely to succeed because of the tight quarters of the valley and ridges on both sides, and the weather was increasingly becoming a factor due to the approach of the monsoon season.

We started to leave the area just as the front of the thunderstorm hit us. We bounced around the sky and finally managed to get away from most of the storm. We always tried our best to avoid large thunderstorms, as the lightning was dangerous and could damage our electronics if the plane were struck. Most of the time we were able to move away because flying in a storm was useless, as you couldn't use the camera system, nor could you do a visual recon, so we learned not to waste our time. We could always go somewhere else and be useful.

15

All Three Landing Gear Wheels Are Supposed to Come Down, Aren't They?

Major Taylor and I were returning to base after completing an uneventful photo/VR mission. The weather was perfect for flying except for the heat and humidity, and we had encountered some small-arms fire, but nothing that caused any undue concern. As we made our normal approach to land at Phu Bai, the major lowered the flaps and adjusted the power and prop levers, and as we approached short final, he pulled the landing gear lever back and we looked at the instrument panel for three green lights indicating that the nose gear and two main gears were down and locked. Two green lights illuminated, and the major tapped the gauge to see whether the third gear light would illuminate. It did not come on, and I looked out of the cockpit at the gear on my side of the plane and was shocked to see it waving in the slipstream. It was hanging there and refused to fully extend and lock into place for landing.

I advised Major Taylor of the situation, and he informed the tower that we had a problem and would have to go around. He applied power and pulled us into a gentle climb out. He raised the gear, and the stubborn gear on my side retracted as it should. The major then pulled the gear lever back to extend the gear, and the wing door opened as I watched and the landing gear came down, but it wouldn't lock into the fully extended position. The major advised the tower of our landing gear problem and also advised the other Mohawk company of our situation. It was decided that several Mohawk pilots would stand near the tower with binoculars, and we would make a slow low-level pass over them, allowing them to look up at our gear to see whether there was any obstruction that I couldn't detect from the cockpit. We made three or four low passes over the other pilots, but they could not see any obstructions or damage.

The major, being an incredible pilot, told me that he was going to get away from the airport and try some strange flight maneuvers. Basically, he told me to hang on and watch the gear and advise him of its movements. The next thing I knew was that we were in a steep climb; then suddenly we were in an extreme right wingover roll. The landing gear followed gravity as the plane rolled and then straightened out and rolled in the other direction. The gear waved from side to side and several times looked as though it would lock into place. However, it continued to be stubborn as the major tried more rolls, loops and other dramatic high- and low-speed turns, climbs and dives. Nothing worked, and now it was time to talk about our options, as our fuel level was starting to become a deciding factor.

The major spoke with some of the other Mohawk pilots on the ground for additional suggestions and to a pilot who was returning to base to land, who flew alongside us to check for damage not visible from the cockpit. He advised that he could not see any damage either. We spoke with the tower about options for landing. Since Phu Bai was a small field, they did not have the equipment to foam the runway if we decided to do a wheels-up landing. They did have fire and rescue trucks and personnel that would assist us if we crashed. We then discussed the only other option, which was to eject from the airplane over the beach near the surf line. In that case, we would have to be careful, because if we did eject near the surf line, we did not want the wind to carry us too far inland and land in a minefield or in the concertina wire. We also did not want to eject too far away from the beach and chance landing in the ocean.

We decided that we would do a wheels-up landing on the runway—simply come in low and slow and pancake the plane on its belly on the runway, and then hang on as it slid down the runway, remembering to disarm the ejection seats just prior to touching down. (Our ejection seats were not designed to be used at extremely low attitudes or while sitting on the ground, as there would not be enough time and altitude for the seat to separate and the parachute to deploy before you slammed into the ground.) We advised the tower of our plan, and they deployed the fire and rescue teams to meet us at the termination of our belly slide.

As we turned toward the airfield, Major Taylor made one last attempt to get the gear to lock into place. He went from level flight to the start of a roll to the left; as he did that, he abruptly rolled to the right, and as I watched, the right main landing gear slammed down as gravity took hold of it and locked into place. The major had performed that roll to the left and then to the right several times during the past hour, but the gear never went down far enough or with enough force to lock into place. We now had three green lights and advised the tower that we were turning into short final and that the fire and rescue teams could relax. I watched the right main gear as we touched down, fully expecting it to collapse as it absorbed the weight of the plane, but it stayed locked in place, and we taxied off the runway to the maintenance area.

16

The Thief at An Khe

Getting around in Vietnam was fairly easy; you just could not be in a great hurry. The few times that I was required to travel from Phu Bai to other locations in Vietnam involved going to the operations building at the airfield and telling whoever was in charge that you wanted transportation to wherever. They would then look at their manifests to see whether any air transportation was going to be available that day or the next. The air transportation could be via a C-130 Hercules, a C-123 (which was like a smaller C-130 with two engines instead of four), a Caribou, or a Huey helicopter (the most likely option). After informing the ops person about your request, you were told to take a seat or stand or sleep on the floor until a transport going to wherever you needed to go became available.

One of the most common destinations for us was the old 1st Cavalry headquarters at An Khe, as that was where all the administrative tasks were performed. The only other really important destination for us was Bien Hoa, and that was used only if you were going on R&R or home. There was an in-country R&R location at Vung Tau where guys would be sent for a week to get them out of the boonies to forget about the war for a few days. (I will describe Vung Tau in detail in another chapter.)

This travel experience was required, as I needed to complete some important paperwork and was told to go to An Khe to sign the documents. I walked from our platoon area at the end of the Phu Bai airfield to the operations building located next to the tower. I walked in and asked for a ride to An Khe. I was told that "probably" I could get on a Huey later in the day; it was then 8:00 a.m., but I was told not to go anywhere, as a ride could become available at any time. I settled down, and about an hour later, an announcement came over the PA system that a Huey was leaving for An Khe, and if you wanted a ride, run out to the tarmac and climb aboard. I did ask the door gunner whether this Huey was headed for An Khe, and he nodded in the affirmative. We had four other passengers on board and headed south to An Khe. The Huey flew at about two thousand feet, and the cooler air felt good blowing through the open vehicle, as this helicopter had its side doors removed (like most of the Hueys in Vietnam).

We had an uneventful ride to An Khe, and when we arrived, I asked for directions to the administration building and walked about a mile to its location. When I arrived, the clerk in charge told me to come back in an hour, as it was lunchtime and everyone was in the mess hall. He told me where it was and to go there for some food. I was hungry, and the food was actually OK in comparison to the mess hall food and C-rations that I normally ate in Phu Bai. I returned to the administration building and completed the required paperwork, after which I left for the airfield and a return flight to Phu Bai. "No more flights going north today," I was told, but I could spend the night in the transit building that was located about half a mile away toward the green line. "Come back first thing in the morning and we'll get you on a flight back to Phu Bai." I thanked the ops guy and headed for the transit hooch but first went to the mess hall for dinner, as it was now close to 6:00 p.m.

I ate and talked with some grunts and other people for a couple of hours and then headed for the transit hooch. The hooch was a good-sized building with about twenty over-and-under bunks, each one with a thin mattress and a small pillow. They were spaced about ten or twelve feet apart, and as I walked into the hooch, a guy stood up, took my name and unit, and told me to pick any bunk that I wanted. He was evidently the hooch commander. There were about six or eight other transit guys already settled in, and I picked a top bunk away from them, as I was tired and didn't want to do any more talking. I was traveling lightly, with only my toothbrush and toothpaste and my Smith & Wesson .38-caliber revolver.

As I walked around the bunk, I noticed some damage to the cement floor of the hooch that had been recently repaired and asked the hooch commander about it. "That is where the satchel charge went off when the sappers threw it in here; luckily, it was a small one, or it would have blown this whole place apart. It only wounded two or three people," he explained as he used his hands to animate the satchel charge being thrown in and blowing up the bunks that were there. He continued, "You don't have to worry about that happening again, 'cause that is why I am here," as he patted his M-16. "I will be right outside the door all night to keep any sappers from blowing anything up." I looked at the guy and somehow did not feel relieved that he was going to prevent anything from getting into the hooch that night. There was a reason that he was assigned as hooch commander, and I did not want to know that reason.

Lights out, but I could not sleep, as An Khe did not sleep at night; there was continuous noise from outgoing artillery, occasionally incoming mortar and rocket explosions, and many Hueys taking off and landing. Finally, around 2:00 a.m., I fell into a restless sleep. I was sleeping on my stomach with my hand under my pillow; also under the pillow was my .38 and wallet. It was pitch black, except for the light from the artillery flashes and the lightning from an approaching thunderstorm, when I suddenly came wide awake, feeling the presence of someone standing very close to my head. I didn't move or even breathe as I determined my next move. My right hand was under my pillow, and I slowly grasped the butt of my .38; as I did that, I felt a slight movement at the edge of my pillow as a hand started to slide under the pillow. I didn't know whether this person had a knife and was going to slit my throat or try to strangle me. All I knew was that I wasn't going to let either of those things happen to me. I readied myself and grasped my .38; then I pulled it out from under my pillow, whirled around, cocked the revolver, and pointed it at the guy's forehead with my finger on the trigger. I growled at the guy, "Don't move a muscle; don't even blink, or I will blow your brains out." The guy screamed, "Don't shoot, don't shoot, please don't shoot!" The noise that the guy made awakened all of the other transit hooch guys, and someone turned on the lights. The scene that unfolded was me lying in my bunk with a guy standing next to my head with a Smith & Wesson .38 revolver cocked and pointed at his forehead. The guy stood there sobbing, "Don't shoot, don't shoot, I'm sorry, I'm sorry." I yelled, "Get the MPs before I shoot this bastard!"

The noise coming from the hooch alerted the guys on guard duty, and they, along with the hooch commander and two MPs, rushed into the hooch. They grabbed the other guy and told me to put my gun away and asked whether he had my wallet. He didn't have a chance to get it, as I had reacted quickly enough to foil his plans. I was told that there had been a lot of thefts from the transit hooch, and this guy admitted to them. He was a druggie and stole wallets and watches, and he would have grabbed my .38 if my sixth sense hadn't warned me of his presence. You do develop a sixth sense in certain situations that definitely warns or awakens you to danger; it happened more times than I can count. I didn't bother trying to get any additional sleep that night; instead, I went outside and watched the thunderstorm.

After breakfast, I walked to the ops building and requested a ride to Phu Bai and was told that I should come back at noon, when there should be a ride available. The 1st Cavalry base at Ah Khe was huge, and I decided to take a walk and look around. I watched helicopters take off and land for a while and saw a road that led toward a small hill. I decided that hill would be a nice spot for watching all the airfield activity, and someone said that the town was not far away. I had plenty of time and decided that a walk into town might be interesting because I had never been in a Vietnamese town. I didn't know how far away the town was, but the day was nice—not scalding hot, but very humid as usual.

As I walked along the road, it slowly dawned on me that I was the only person on the road and that the jungle was closing in at an alarming rate on my right side and I was only armed with a .38-caliber revolver. As I studied the jungle, I wondered, "What if a stray sniper was hiding in the trees and he noticed this fool all alone and apparently unarmed and decided that I would make a nice trophy?" As I mulled this idea over, I heard the noise of an approaching vehicle; before I could wave at them, they sped up and stopped next to me and said, "Get in before a sniper gets you; what are you doing walking out here?" Before I could reply, they sped away and told me not to ever go for a walk like that again and dropped me off at the ops building. The timing was perfect, as a Huey arrived earlier than expected and I climbed aboard, glad to be returning to Phu Bai.

As I watched the terrain pass by under the helicopter, I thought about what had happened and how I had come so close to blowing that thief away. Had he moved or tried to fight me, I would have pulled the trigger, but I was immensely thankful that he had not done anything and even more grateful that I had not overreacted. I then thought about the road walk I had taken and kicked myself for being so careless and not considering my surroundings along that deserted road and the potential consequences. Sometimes you get exceptionally lucky or whatever.

I was at Camp Evans (the new 1st Cavalry headquarters) for some reason and had to spend the night, as there were not any additional flights that day going to Phu Bai. I was told that I could bunk in a tent with some helicopter crewmembers and use an empty bunk that belonged to a guy who was away on R&R. I agreed, and when lights out came, I went to the guy's bunk. Well, don't ever use anyone else's bunk, as you don't know what is living in and under the poncho liner or in the sleeping bag. The stench coming from that bunk was similar to the first breath of air that I experienced getting off the 707 after arriving in Bien Hoa. I stood there and retched as a couple of other guys who lived at the far end of the tent commented on the individual's bunk that I was supposed to use that night. "No way in hell," I said out loud, "am I going anywhere near that guy's bunk; hasn't anyone ever told him to wash his poncho liner once in a while or air out his sleeping bag?" I sat down on an empty ammo box and resigned myself to yet another night without sleep.

I must have dozed off while sitting on the box, as the next thing I was aware of was the noise of a large explosion that peppered the tent with debris, resulting in guys running in all directions yelling, "Incoming!" I didn't know which way to go to get to a bunker and stood there until someone grabbed me by the shoulder and shoved me out of the tent and toward a bunker. We stayed in the bunker for about ten minutes while listening to machine-gun and small-arms fire and numerous other explosions. Finally, everything settled down, and we exited the bunker and watched as numerous flares illuminated the night sky at the edge of the green line. The attack had broken off, and everyone relaxed again. I went back to the edge of the bunker and watched the flares until they burned out. I then sat on an empty ammo box and waited for daybreak and a ride back to Phu Bai and a daytime photo/VR mission that was sure to be accompanied by incoming tracers and other small-arms fire.

Traveling around Vietnam via helicopter was usually uneventful; it just took some time and patience to travel from one location to another. There were no set schedules, and sometimes to get from one point to another you had to detour and then wait there for a flight going in your direction. One day I was trying to return to Phu Bai from somewhere and was advised that the next helicopter landing would be going in that direction with one stop. "No problem," I said. I should have looked around before I said "no problem" because as the helicopter approached to land, a very large Vietnamese family eased onto the tarmac with all of their personal items. These people were voluntarily relocating to be with other family members, and the government and the U.S. Army had committed to help them move by loading them onto a Huey. The family now loaded onto the helicopter included grandparents, parents, several young children, two infants, two goats and two baskets of chickens and a rooster along with whatever personal items they could carry.

Needless to say, the helicopter was now fully loaded, and it was the only one out of there until sometime the next day or the day after. I looked at the pilots and at a door gunner, who shrugged his shoulders and pointed at an open space on the floor next to his left foot. I sat down but could not get any farther inside the helicopter. I placed both feet on the left skid and pushed backward but was thwarted in my attempt to get any farther inside the helicopter by livestock and a pile of personal items. The door gunner looked down at me and indicated that this was best they could do if I wanted to fly that day. I turned around and looked at the loaded helicopter, then down at my feet resting on the skids, and then at the gunner, who told me that the flight with the Vietnamese family would be only twenty minutes or less. There was nothing to hang on to, and I leaned as far back into the helicopter as I could; even then, I was still pitched outward. On this flight I had borrowed McMann's M-16 and rested the butt of the rifle on the skid and used it as a crutch to help stabilize my precarious situation.

The door gunner gave me the thumbs-up sign and the pilots increased power, and we lifted off in the typical Huey nose-down fashion. We quickly gained altitude and cruised at 2,500 feet over the terrain below. The midday weather was clear and hot, but the breeze blowing past the helicopter helped clear the inside of the helicopter of the smell of the livestock. Suddenly the helicopter pitched to the left, lifting me off the floor until I was actually standing upright on the left skid and pitching forward off the helicopter; I pushed harder with the M-16 on the skid for balance when the door gunner grabbed the back of my shirt and held me there as he spoke to the pilot, who immediately swung the chopper back to the right, putting my butt back down on the floor. The pilots had taken evasive action because of incoming ground fire and now eased back to more stable flight. I continued to press my feet against the skid and pushed back as hard as I could to stay away from that open space.

We flew for another ten minutes until I saw a hamlet below us. The pilot headed for an open space near the hamlet and set the chopper down gently. The Vietnamese family couldn't wait to exit, and within seconds they and their livestock were running toward their relatives in the hamlet. The door gunners took a minute to sweep out the floor of the helicopter; finally, the gunner who had grabbed my shirt looked at me and said, "Just because you have wings on your shirt doesn't mean that you can fly; next time try to stay inside the helicopter." Then he laughed and pushed me onto a seat *inside* the chopper. We lifted off and headed for Phu Bai, which was about an hour away. I wished I had my flight helmet, as I would have liked to plug into their communications system and listen to their conversation. We landed, and I got off the chopper and headed in the wrong direction—I was caught before I could walk toward the tail rotor and directed to walk along the fuselage toward the front and side of the helicopter, and then walk away from the side of it.

Another time I was going somewhere in Vietnam and needed a ride. I got a helicopter ride from Phu Bai to a bigger airfield, where I thought that I would find another Huey ride, but was told that another airplane would arrive shortly that was going where I needed to go and that a platoon of grunts was going to come too. A platoon of fully loaded grunts would need five Hueys to carry them and their gear, so the arriving airplane had to be something else to carry all of us at once. I imagined a C-130 or maybe a Chinook helicopter—those could carry all of us and more easily.

The plane we were waiting for soon became visible, and I could see that it looked like a C-130, but it had only two engines, not four, and was considerably smaller. It was a C-123, a small cousin of the C-130. It landed and taxied to a parking spot; the rear ramp lowered, and several people emerged and went into the operations building. The plane sat there with its engines running, and I noticed that on either side of the fuselage behind the wings and toward the rear there was a jet engine mounted—one on each side. I asked about them, and a crewmember told me that the jet engines were called JATO (jet-assisted take off) engines. These were used when the plane was fully loaded or when taking off from a short runway. I said, "Oh, are they loud?" The crew member replied by pointing at the ear protection headset that he wore. About this time, the grunts saddled up, and I followed them up the ramp into the inside of the airplane. It was empty except for us, and I wondered whether the JATO engines would be used.

As soon as everyone sat on the floor, the ramp came up and the plane started to move. We taxied rather quickly to the end of the runway, and before we were cleared for takeoff, I heard two jet engines very close to us spool up. I said, "Crap," and stuck my fingers in my ears. The two turboprop engines cranked up, and the plane shuddered as it strained against the brakes. The brakes were released, and we started to roll when the JATOs were fully activated, and the additional thrust could be easily felt. The plane gathered speed quicker than I thought, and as soon as the wheels came up, we went into a steep climb, the JATOs really adding their thrust to our ascent. The airplane was noisy, as you would expect a hollow freight-carrying airplane to be, but we had a smooth ride and landed without experiencing any problems. I walked off with the grunts, asked directions and completed my business. Later that afternoon, I caught a Huey back to Phu Bai. That was the only time that I ever flew on a C-123, and I decided that once was enough.

17

The Big Move South

Early December 1968, the entire 1st Cavalry Division was ordered out of I Corps and directed to deploy in III Corps near Saigon. The entire division packed everything in Camp Evans and An Khe and moved south to Phuoc Vinh to guard Saigon against NVA excursions from Cambodia. We were told to pack our meager personal items in a box and label it with our name. The box would then be placed in one of our three vehicles (the major's jeep, our deuce and a half, and a five-quarter-ton truck), which would be driven south on Highway 1 to Vung Tau, where we were assigned with our six Mohawks to share the airfield with another Mohawk unit, the 73rd Aviation Company. We would have our own platoon area but use their mess hall and other facilities, except we would maintain our own club.

Most of the guys in the platoon loaded on our three vehicles, but a few of us were lucky enough to fly to Vung Tau in our Mohawks. Major Taylor took me with him in one of our C model infrared ships, and we flew down the coast to Vung Tau. The flight was spectacular, with the ocean, beach and islands appearing below us, and no one shot at us—a first-time experience flying in Vietnam. When we got near Vung Tau, a rather large town or small city appeared. It was located at the mouth of the Saigon River with a large seaport and fishing boat fleet and oceanfront on the east side of the city, with a large hill topped with a lighthouse indicating the location of the river mouth. As we cruised over the area, I noticed a large freighter that was bow first on the beach to the left of the river entrance. I never found out why it was beached there, as it didn't seem to have noticeable damage, but it served as a tourist attraction.

When we landed, we were directed to the end of the taxiway away from the other Mohawk company's airplanes. We parked as directed, and a jeep met us and took us to an area several hundred yards from our airplanes. We were told this was our new platoon area; the enlisted men would have two-man rooms in the hooches, and the pilots would have quarters in a hotel in town. The rooms in the hooches were a fantastic change after living in a leaking tent for six months. We even had a building with shower stalls, cement floors, sturdy walls and flush toilets.

Hooches in Vung Tau. Mine was on the far end.

The rest of the platoon personnel arrived three days later, and I was given McMann (famous for chasing rats with my .38) as my roommate. We had bunk beds, and I chose the top bunk, thinking that maybe I would somehow be in a better airflow than being closer to the floor. The first night or morning in Vung Tau, McMann had gotten up early to repair something on one of our ships, and I was rudely awakened by the voices of Vietnamese who were right outside my room. Startled, I grabbed my .38 and rushed out the door into the hallway and nearly stepped on four mama-sans who were squatting on the floor shining jungle boots. They looked up at me standing there in my shorts with a revolver in my hand, appearing completely confused, and smiled at me with their bezel-nut-stained teeth. I tried to clear my head and finally remembered that I was in Vung Tau, where things were done differently. In Phu Bai, the only Vietnamese we had seen was a papa-san who cut our hair. We (that is, the ASTA platoon) did not have any other contact with Vietnamese civilians. The mama-sans had been talking very loudly when I surprised them in the hallway. They had not realized that anyone was still sleeping in the hooch. After the initial surprise meeting and my confused and sleepy look, we all relaxed, and when I panto-mimed sleeping and put my hand over my mouth, they began to whis-per, and I turned around and went back into my room and locked the door.

I found out that everyone living the in the hooches hired the mama-sans to clean the rooms, do laundry and shine their boots—all for about a dollar a week. We of course used MPCs (military payment certificates), as standard U.S. greenbacks were not allowed due to the black market trade for standard U.S. dollars. I signed up there and then for the laundry, boot and hooch cleaning service. I don't know where they washed our clothes but assumed that there was a washing machine somewhere close to the hooches. The clothes always came back clean and fresh smelling, so I reasoned that the mama-sans used clean water, not something else.

That first morning, I tried to get back to sleep, but the heat and humidity were overwhelming, so I got dressed and left to find some food. After chow, I caught a ride to the beach to investigate that beached freighter and check out the waves. The freighter had been there a while, and the surf conditions made it too dangerous to get near it in the water. I walked down the beach, and the water looked inviting, with waves that could be body surfed, but I didn't have a bathing suit and didn't see anyone else in the water—a sure sign that maybe you shouldn't go in. I noticed a building on the beach and went in; it was a mess hall or beach club of sorts, offering T-bone steaks with a baked potato and a green salad and burgers and fries and beer. I looked around at the building, the food, and the beach and said, "Where am I?"

After I left the beach, I went into downtown Vung Tau. There were bars, hotels, restaurants, shops of all kinds, residential homes along the tree-lined streets and along the riverfront, and lots of people coming and going. There were many military people driving and walking around and hordes of civilians going about their business. I found out that the American military units in Vung Tau had claimed various bars as their own turf, and outsiders were not allowed in unless invited.

Next stop was the PX: "Holy cow, this place is unbelievable." This PX, after what we had in Phu Bai, was like a candy shop, electronics store, camera store, upscale clothing store, grocery store, shoe store, hat shop, and (last but not least) automotive dealership dream store. After spending considerable time looking at everything I couldn't afford, I especially wanted a good 35 mm camera to use in the cockpit, but as I couldn't afford even the cheapest one, I settled on a super-cheap Pola-roid camera that took lousy pictures: a waste of money that I didn't have.

After drooling over everything else, I approached the automotive dealership section. Every car manufacturer imaginable had a booth set up with colorful brochures for the taking. Each booth was manned by a knowledgeable representative who was more than happy to write up a new order on the spot. Order the car now, and it would be waiting for you at your local dealership when you arrived home. The choices were mind-boggling, with the Chevy guys drooling over SS 396 Chevelles and Camaros alongside 427 Impalas and Corvettes. The Pontiac guys were crazy for GTOs or Firebirds, while the Dodge guys couldn't wait for their new 389 tri-power Chargers or their 426 Hemi Dodges or Plymouth Road Runners. Oldsmobile got into it with the 442. The Ford guys wanted their 427 Galaxies or 427 Cobras or hi-po Mustangs and Fairlanes. I'm a car guy and liked Fords, but some of the imports caught my eye. How about a Jaguar or Triumph, or possibly a new BMW 2002, or a Swedish brick called a 122 or 140? My God, I wanted to order a new car, but the reality of having no money clobbered me back into the real world. I just looked on as guy after guy signed on the dotted line for his new ride waiting at home for him. Little did I know that after my discharge, I would in fact buy a used BMW 1600—not the 2002 that I wanted but essentially the same car with a smaller engine. Soon after that, I also bought a brand new Swedish brick, a 1971 242, which I kept for ten years.

Later that week, several of us from the 1st Cavalry found a nice bar that was across the street from the river and claimed it for the Cavalry. We were having a beer when several Green Berets walked in, and we asked them to join us. They wanted to know about I Corps, so we told them about our tents, A Shau Valley, the mountains, deep valley fire support bases on mountaintops, and river and trail photo/VR missions, not to forget our nightly infrared and SLAR missions and other experiences dealing with the Navy and the Marines.

As time went on, several of us found a Chinese restaurant on the second floor of a nice hotel. The food was excellent and the owner liked us, as we went there quite often. One day when we walked in, he took us aside, as the restaurant was nearly full, and leaned forward and whispered, "Chicken say meow, meow today." Needless to say, none of us had chicken that day; it was shrimp all around.

Somehow, we found ourselves with some free time during the day, and we often went to the beach, but it was so hot on the sand that all you could do was go for a quick dip and head for the shade. The other free-time fun was to go into town, find our favorite bar and have a cold beer. One day, while walking around town looking at the various shops, one caught my eye—a Hong Kong tailor shop. Everything they sold was custom made, and you were measured by the tailor, ensuring that whatever piece of clothing you purchased fit you perfectly. Suits, shirts and pants were their specialty. You were shown bolts of cloth from which you chose the fabric and color, and then you stood on a platform and the tailor measured you from head to toe to create a perfectly fitting suit. This shop, in addition to the suit, included two custom-made silk shirts and a matching tie. I finally decided on a fabric and color and ordered my custom-made suit, just like James Bond, which was a perfect fit when I picked it up a week later. However, because of my weight loss, the suit only fit me for a very short time when I returned home, and I should have chosen a more traditional color instead of the blue that I selected at the time. I should have asked the tailor, when he measured me, to add a few pounds to the overall size of the suit and shirts.

My roommate McMann thought that our room was too hot and the thin mattresses were uncomfortable, so he left to do something about our living conditions. I soon left to go on a VR (visual recon) mission, followed by an all-night infrared mission, not returning until morning. The next morning was especially hot and humid, and as I entered the hooch, I heard a whirring noise coming from the room McMann and I shared. On entering the room, I was almost blown over from the force of a fan—not just a table fan, but the kind that you find in a mess hall that is six feet tall with two-and-a-half-foot-long fan blades. McMann was nowhere to be found, and as I stared at the fan, I glanced toward the bunk beds, and on each bed was a brand new mattress that was at least six inches thick. "Holy crap, where did McMann find these or, more precisely, who did he steal these from?" I guess I really didn't want to know or care, as I made myself comfortable on my new mattress after adjusting the air flow from our new fan. McMann never told me, and all I know is that the MPs never arrested him.

Late one afternoon I was reading in my room in the hooch when someone close by fired several rounds from his .45 Colt pistol. The shots came from the hooch next to mine, and I grabbed my .38 and ran out to see what was happening. Several other guys came running from different directions, and we stood at the hooch door with our guns drawn, not knowing what to expect. After a few seconds passed, a voice from inside the hooch called out, "Everything is OK, you can come in." We filed into the hooch and looked into the first room and saw several pockmarks on the cement floor where the .45-caliber rounds had impacted. We said, "What the hell is going on?" The guy who lived there told us that he was napping and felt something crawling on his leg; when he looked, there was a three-inch-long (or longer) cockroach crawling on him. He told us that he knocked the cockroach off his leg onto the floor, where he threw his boot at it as it crawled back toward his bunk. He then noticed several more cockroaches approaching his bunk, and he tried to hit them with his other boot, but they kept coming. Panicking, he grabbed his .45 and shot several times at the cockroaches. Those were the gunshots that everyone had heard.

Another person entered the hooch room—a senior NCO who had heard the entire story and grabbed the .45 from the guy and put him on report for firing a weapon inside a hooch. Several of us discussed the incident and concluded that the guy (who was known to smoke stuff) probably hallucinated the entire cockroach scenario, but he could have killed someone with ricocheting rounds. The guy was court-martialed, demoted and placed on ugly details until he left for home.

Don was another crew chief and considered himself an audiophile, as he had recently gone to the PX in Vung Tau and purchased stereo equipment complete with speakers that could blow the walls off his hooch. He lived in one of the two-story hooches with an open floorplan. He was hooking up his new audio equipment and was going to impress us with the sound and volume quality. He was in the process of running speaker wire to his speakers from the subwoofer and receiver while five or six of us watched. These two-story hooches had exposed rafters, and with bunk beds in place, if you stood on the top bunk, you could reach the rafters. This was exactly what Don did to bring the wires over the rafters to his speakers, which he was going to mount in the rafters. The only thing he forgot was that the two-story hooches had metal-bladed overhead fans to move the air around, and if you stood up on top of the upper bunk, you could get hit in the head by one of the slowly turning fan blades. Don stood up, and as he draped his speaker wire over a rafter, he leaned into one of the fan blades, which caught him on the top side of his head. He wasn't hurt, but the blade caused a nasty cut, which bled like crazy. We helped him down off the top bunk and wrapped his head in a towel as we laughed our heads off at his expense.

We loaded Don in a jeep and rushed to the field hospital, where the doctors and nurses thought that he had been shot in the head because of the amount of blood soaking through the towel. We were still laughing when we handed him over to the medical people, who looked at us like we were crazy. "What the hell is so funny?" one of the doctors demanded. "We will tell you as soon as you take care of him," we said. A doctor and two nurses disappeared behind a curtain with Don, and soon we heard him yelling, "Don't shave my head!" You see, Don was hair conscious and never wanted a hair out of place; for him to get his head shaved was too much to take. He yelled and pleaded and almost threatened (but he didn't, as these were officers working on him and he didn't want to be sent to the stockade, so he sat there and steamed). When they finished with him, Don had a shaved head and several stiches and a huge bandage around his head. He looked like he was wearing a turban. He buried his head the best he could in his hat, but the large bandage on his head could not be covered by his hat, and that only made us laugh harder. Finally, the doctor and nurses had enough of our antics and asked again what had happened, as Don would not tell them. We recounted the entire story, and they had to turn their backs to us as they snickered (not as quietly as they should have) and disappeared behind the curtain only to return and tell us to bring Don back the next day to have the bandage changed. Don did get his speakers wired and would not remove his hat in front of anyone for at least two weeks.

Another time three of us entered a bar in an area of Vung Tau that we had not seen before. It was an OK area, but not as nice as most of the city, and we were the only non–Vietnamese in this section of the city. We noticed the lack of military vehicles and thought it was a tad strange, because the rest of the city was full of military trucks and jeeps. There was also a strange lack of civilians going about their business. There were a few civilians walking around, but not the large numbers we saw elsewhere. It was extremely hot, and when we saw the bar, we didn't think twice about entering to have a cold beer. When we entered, however, we noticed that we were the only Americans in the bar, which was unusual, and the bar was full of Vietnamese males. As we entered, all conversation stopped. We sat a table near the doorway and observed the Vietnamese examining us. The Army had a rule that firearms were not allowed in the city of Vung Tau except for official business; therefore, we were not armed except for a jack-knife that each of us carried. The bar patrons seated at tables and at the bar appeared to become very uneasy, and their discomfort increased when a mama-san came up to us, pointed at our Cavalry patches and said loudly, "1st Cav. numba ten, no numba ten thou," which means bad—very bad.

We thought better of ordering beer when we looked more closely at the Vietnamese men in the bar. Their legs from the knee down were covered with scratches and dried blood. Usually, someone who spends his time working in a rice paddy would not have scratches like those that we observed. We noticed some movement at the other tables and took that as an invitation to *didi mau* (get the hell out of there). We got up and quickly left, as we were outnumbered ten or more to one, and headed back to familiar areas. We were followed for a short distance by a number of the bar patrons, who made it clear that they didn't want us back in that area. As I mentioned earlier, Vung Tau was an in-country R&R center for all parties involved in combat in Vietnam, and we had just intruded on a bar full of VC and NVA. We were very lucky that it was daytime, not night, as we would not have made it out of that bar alive.

Later that afternoon, MPs stopped me and asked me where my hat was (you were out of uniform if you weren't wearing your hat); I responded that it was either in a bar full of Viet Cong or in the A Shau Valley—either way, I was not going back for it. They pointed at a shop across the street and told me to go there and buy a new hat. I did.

My new aviator sunglasses, made by the American Optical Company in Massachusetts.

18

Haka

Please do a Google or YouTube search for "haka" and click on a video of either the New Zealand national rugby team (the All Blacks) or a military unit performing a haka, and you will have a better understanding of what I am about to describe. First, though, I will share with you an explanation given to me by an Aussie grunt and his Maori mates about what a haka is and how and when a haka is used. A haka is an ancient Maori tribal ceremonial dance that celebrates life, death, challenges, hardship, determination, respect, admiration, service and survival. There are hakas that celebrate important events in life, such as marriage, funerals, retirements, and official visits from dignitaries; most important, hakas are used to show respect to an individual, team or fallen comrades. The most common or well-known haka was a war dance haka, Ka Mate, the purpose of which was to intimidate opponents while at the same time respecting and honoring them for the courage they displayed in standing up to the group performing the haka. It is considered extremely disrespectful if the opponents do not stand there and appreciate the haka that is directed at them, refraining from mimicking or making light of the haka. There are videos of high school students—every student in the school—performing a haka for a retiring teacher whom they admired and respected.

All New Zealand sports teams perform a haka prior to their particular game or match. Every team, from rugby to field hockey, basketball, ice hockey, water polo and everything else, both men's and women's teams, performs a haka in front of their adversaries. This includes high school and college teams. These particular hakas are a combination of challenge and intimidation, as well as a show of respect for the other team, in addition to psyching up the team performing the haka. Every haka is led by a leader, who starts the chant, with the other members chanting in unison while performing synchronized body movements, moving slowly forward toward their opponents while shouting and making gestures like puffing out their cheeks and bulging out their eyes, culminating in the final insult—sticking out their tongues while making savage facial expressions.

One of the most moving hakas was performed by a military unit at a funeral for three of their comrades who were killed by an IED while serving in Iraq or Afghanistan. I have never witnessed such admiration and respect for fellow fallen soldiers as I saw in this video.

It was nearly New Year's Eve, and several of us were sitting in our bar in downtown Vung Tau, which was frequented only by 1st Cavalry troopers and Green Beret troops. All the GIs in the Vung Tau area were very territorial and claimed certain bars as their own and would not generally allow other GIs to intrude on their turf. We 1st Cavalry troopers claimed a particular bar that was across from the waterfront river area but allowed Green Berets to share it with us. We also welcomed the Aussies and Kiwis. An Aussie squad of grunts entered; they were at their compound on the beach in Vung Tau for some in-country R&R and came into town for some local flavor. We all got along well, especially after several beers. (We generally had a Vietnamese beer named Bah Me Bah, which translates to "thirty-three." Why that name, no one knows; maybe it only contained 3.3 percent alcohol—we never found out.)

Since New Year's Eve was only a day later, we invited the Aussie grunts and Kiwis to join us at our compound for a New Year's Eve celebration. They accepted, and we exchanged names so that we didn't have to say "hey you" when we wanted to say something. The squad leader said his name was Ellen, and I thought it was a tad strange for a guy to have a girl's name, but I let it go and called him Ellen. One of the other Aussies looked at me after I called Ellen "Ellen" and told me that I had a great Australian accent. "What do you mean?" I asked. "His name is spelled A-L-A-N, but in Australia it is pronounced Ellen," replied the Aussie. Crap, did I feel stupid as I repeated his name with an American pronunciation. Everyone had heard me calling him Ellen and laughed like crazy when I changed to the American pronunciation.

Around 9:30 p.m. on New Year's Eve, about ten Aussie and Kiwi grunts were dropped off at our platoon area (Vung Tau bars were off limits on New Year's Eve), and all of us began to drink, tell jokes and stories about home and Vietnam and just have a good time. I wasn't much of a drinker and had two or three beers; I didn't like hard liquor, so before long I was the only person in that club who could not only see straight but also walk and chew gum without falling. Finally, at about 3:00 a.m., I asked Alan what time he and his group had to be back at their compound. He slurred a reply, and I asked him again. This time he said they would be AWOL if they weren't signed in at their compound by 1:00 a.m. "Oh, shit," I thought; it was already after 3:00 a.m.

I had to get them back to their compound before they were discovered missing.

I quickly devised a plan that was, in my opinion, foolproof. All we had to do was load everyone into the bed of our deuce and a half, and I would drive them back to their compound via the beach and then off the beach to their hooch. Incredible plan, if I do say so myself. What could go wrong with ten superbly drunk Aussies and eight or ten incredibly drunk Americans all piled into the bed of an Army truck that was to be driven on the beach and into an Aussie compound? Not to mention high tide and Aussie MP jeeps equipped with quad .50-caliber machine guns. We had a wonderful time loading numerous drunk Aussies and Americans who wanted to come along for the ride. Luckily, we didn't have to tie anyone down so they wouldn't fall out of the truck. They were so drunk that once on the truck, they just sat there leaning against each other.

Now to put my plan into motion. I was able to exit the main gate of the airfield and head toward town, but I knew that there would be a roadblock ahead; that was OK, as I was going to turn off the main road and head for the beach. There was no one around as I eased onto the beach sand and headed for the Aussie compound that was less than a mile away. I noticed that the tide was coming in, so I turned away from the waves and headed for a road that ran parallel to the shoreline, thinking that I would not drive on that road but stay on the beach and drive directly into the Aussie compound via the beach route.

All was going well; I had not lost anyone off the truck, but I soon realized that my plan was not perfect. In the headlights of the truck, I saw rolls and rolls of concertina wire extending from out of the ocean across the beach in front of me and continuing to the light jungle and road. The only choice I had was to get off the beach and onto the road leading to the Aussie compound. I had accomplished that and was happily motoring along when suddenly the road in front of me became as bright as midday. I had found two Aussie MP jeeps that had been sitting on the road listening to my approach. A diesel deuce and a half is not a quiet truck. The jeeps were equipped with very powerful searchlights and blinded me as I came to a stop. The Aussie jeeps approached slowly with the searchlights illuminated, and a gruff Aussie sergeant came to my door as I was climbing out of the truck. Several additional Aussie MPs came up to the truck and walked around it while peering with flashlights into the bed of the truck. "What is going on?" the MP barked at me. He walked to the rear of the truck with me as he and the other MPs looked at the tangle of drunk bodies loaded onto the truck. I explained that we had invited the grunts to celebrate New Year's Eve with us at our platoon club and that time had gotten away from us and I was simply bringing them home. I said, "Look, Sarge, this is all my fault. I didn't check the time, and I didn't want these guys getting into any trouble, so I tried to bring them back via the beach; they were with us all the time and not in town." I continued, "They needed to burn off stress and get away from the memory of the boonies, so they came to our club to unwind." He looked at me and then at the happy drunks and said, "Follow us with your truck." I asked him again whether these guys were in trouble; he shook his head and said, "No because all of you mates were on your compound together."

I followed the lead jeep, and the second followed me to make sure that no one fell off the truck. We stopped at a hooch and unloaded any Australian or New Zealander we could find and discovered that there were none missing. As they staggered into the hooch, assisted by the MPs, Alan said, "Thanks for the lift and the party; we need you mates to come back here today around 6:00 p.m. for steak and beer and shrimp on the barbie." I looked at the head MP and thanked him for not shooting us and for letting us bring his mates home. He nodded his head and pointed at the main gate and said, "See you mates later for steaks and beer."

At 6:00 that evening, we entered the Aussie/Kiwi compound via the main gate in our deuce and a half and parked near the mess hall. Our hosts had a huge bonfire blazing and beautiful steaks cooking on the barbecue. A second and third barbecue held shrimp and chicken and probably lamb. The aroma was fantastic, and we drew in deep breaths to savor the moment. Alan came out of the mess hall carrying Foster's brand Aussie beer in cans that were the size of quart oil cans. The beer was fresh and very cold. There were eight Americans and a much larger number of Aussies and Kiwis gathered around the barbecue grills and bonfire, toasting each other and wishing everyone a Happy New Year. We all sat at large picnic tables that were placed on the sand about one hundred feet from the waves and thoroughly enjoyed the cooling sea breeze. We sat there drinking our Foster's and gazed out to sea; it was very peaceful, and everyone became totally relaxed until the grill masters said these magic words: "Medium rare is ready." We stood up as one and descended on those grills, loading our plates with huge, thick steaks and shrimp and chicken. There were fresh vegetables and freshly baked bread and rolls as well as more Foster's. We ate and drank until we saw the desserts and applied ourselves to cakes, cookies and pies, all freshly baked. We were so satisfied and content that all we could do was sit there and look at the breaking waves and imagine that this beach was located somewhere other than Vietnam.

As the sun set and darkness slowly descended on us, I noticed that most of the Kiwis had risen from the tables and moved toward the far side of the bonfire. There were perhaps twenty of them, and they began to take off their uniforms until they stood near the bonfire dressed in their shorts and bare feet. Almost all of them were Maori tribesmen. Someone added more driftwood to the bonfire, and it grew to a considerable size. Suddenly, one of the Kiwis yelled something very loudly, and the rest of the Kiwis assumed an aggressive stance, with their feet wide apart and their knees bent and their upper bodies bent forward from the waist. Their leader yelled another command, and the entire group, with a very loud voice, chanted in unison while slapping their thighs and then their chests. I said to Alan, "What is going on?" He smiled and looked at me and said, "They are going to scare the living shit out of you, mate."

At that comment, as if on cue, the Maori leader yelled something else, and the entire group chanted in unison, slapping their thighs and chests, all while making hideous faces. They slapped their biceps and forearms, still chanting, and suddenly started moving forward, but because of the bonfire, they had to move sideways and then forward with slow deliberate steps accompanied by a stomping of their feet. If the bonfire had not been in the way, they would have moved directly toward us. You could feel the electricity in the air as these warriors performed their haka for us. They continued to chant in unison and used their bodies in synchronicity as they got closer and closer. Finally, when they were ten or fifteen feet from us, they said one last chant and bulged out their eyes and cheeks while sticking out their tongues and chanted one final word that sounded like "hi" or "he" shouted in unison.

This was unbelievable; none of us had ever seen anything like this display for getting ready for battle. We had to have another Foster's with these guys as we asked them question after question about what we had just seen and experienced. They proudly explained the story behind the "Ka Mate" haka they had just performed and how it really was a proclamation of life triumphing over death and of escape and salvation. It was composed by a Maori chieftain who was pursued by enemies and hidden by a friendly tribe who convinced the pursuers to leave. The chieftain, after realizing he was not going to die, composed this haka for his saviors.

The haka performed for us has many facets: it is used to psych up the warriors performing the haka, preparing them for the upcoming conflict; to cause uncertainty among their foes; and to show respect for their foes in having the courage to confront the haka-performing tribe. Our haka was performed as a sign of respect for our mutual combat service in Vietnam. When we were informed of all of this, we were humbled and expressed our gratitude and appreciation for their respect and the honor they gave us. After all that, we had to toast them with at least one more Foster's.

It was after 11:00 p.m. when the bonfire had burned down and we had run out of conversation topics and energy, so we headed back to our area. We never got together with the Aussies/Kiwis again, as they were only on a week-long in-country R&R and had to get back to the boonies somewhere in Vietnam. Those of us who experienced that night were profoundly impressed by the living culture expressed by those Maori tribesmen of New Zealand.

19

Guard Duty, Vung Tau Style

We had been in Vung Tau for about two weeks when we were told that it was our turn to pull guard duty, along with a group from the 73rd Aviation Company, another large Mohawk unit. Being in the 1st Cavalry and recently arrived from I Corps, we were used to guard duty being performed like your life depended on being prepared, since in reality it was. I was the ranking guy, and seven of us walked (not marched) to the 73rd's company area to receive our guard duty assignments. As we rounded the corner, we were startled by the sight presented to us. There in front of us, in a military formation, stood twenty-five guys wearing starched fatigues and spit-shined boots, with no helmets or flak jackets, and each guy held an M-14 rifle with one magazine of bullets. It reminds me today of the old Andy Griffith show where he gave his deputy, Barney Fife, one bullet for his revolver.

When we came around the corner, walking rather than marching, we were laughed at because of our appearance. Each one of us, due to our previous guard duty experiences, carried the following: an M-16 rifle, two bandoliers of twenty rounds per magazine, ten or twelve magazines per bandolier, and several hand grenades hanging from our flak vests. A few of us had smoke grenades hanging from our vests in addition to the hand grenades, and those on flight status had our .38 revolvers in a holster on a belt around our waist. Our fatigues were generally clean but would have fallen apart if anyone tried to starch them; our boots were well-worn jungle boots that had never seen polish. We were for the most part clean shaven, and a couple of us had recent haircuts—not the short military style, but haircuts nonetheless.

We walked to an area next to the other group, and a lieutenant walked over to us and called us to attention. I had flown several times with him and thought he was a good guy. He stood in front of me and assessed the group standing before him. He looked at me, the M-16 I held, the bandoliers of ammunition, the hand grenades, the flak vest, my helmet, and my revolver. Before he could say anything, I said to him,

"This is how we went on guard duty where we came from." He looked at me again and said, "Next time at least put some polish on your boots." I said, "Yes, sir," and he looked at my M-16 (which was actually McMann's) and asked to inspect the weapon. I handed it to him, and he pulled back the bolt, looked at the receiver and handed it back to me. He walked away toward the other group, and I wondered what he was thinking. I decided that I would ask him the next time we flew together.

The guy in charge of the guard duty group and I were the same rank, and he was also from Massachusetts, which gave us a sense of bonding, and he gave me a cherry guard duty assignment. I was to stand in a guard shack at the entrance to a large hotel located in the heart of Vung Tau, which served as an in-country R&R hotel. All I had to do was keep non-R&R troops out of the hotel. The vast majority of the hotel guests were grunts who were sent out of the field for a week away from the jungle carnage to enjoy a real city with an oceanfront beach, nightlife, bars, tailor shops, restaurants and a fully stocked PX where they could purchase stereo equipment, cameras and whatever else was needed.

I was the only one assigned to this spot, and my shift was a full twelve-hour one that would last until 6:00 a.m. The hotel and grounds were well lighted, as was the city of Vung Tau. It was well known that Vung Tau was also the in-country R&R site for Viet Cong and NVA troops. Generally, everything was well controlled by both sides, and we did not expect any problems, as this city was too important to all parties concerned to mess things up with any kind of confrontation.

Everything was going well until a full bird colonel with his entourage approached my guard shack, and because I was watching some drunk GIs approach, I didn't see him until he was nearly at my post. He instantly called me to attention and wanted to know why I hadn't saluted him. I quickly pointed to the group of grunts approaching us and told the colonel that I was concerned about them getting run over by the military and civilian traffic on the road next to us. The colonel and his entire group now turned their attention to the grunts as they staggered toward us and the gate entrance to the R&R hotel. As we watched, all of the grunts stopped in their tracks and, almost in unison, started to vomit up the copious amounts of alcohol that they had consumed. The colonel looked at them, looked at me, noticed my Cavalry patch and asked whether I had just arrived in the area. I told him that I had recently arrived and that this was my first guard duty away from action. He looked at the group of grunts, then at me, and said, "Good luck." He and his group quickly left for their jeeps and their own hotel, restaurant and (more important) bar. The drunk and sick grunts got themselves together and entered the hotel grounds and headed for the swimming pool. Luckily for me, they were at least a hundred feet from my position when they unloaded their alcohol.

The evening grew quiet, as there was a curfew and all military personnel had to be off the streets and either out of town or in their hotels by 10:00 p.m. Usually there was a strong military police presence to enforce the curfew, but that night I didn't see any MPs drive by the R&R hotel. As the evening drew on, the streets began to come alive with several Vietnamese teenage males riding motor scooters. They were up to no good and raced up and down the streets, throwing things and yelling at me. They were in the street drinking and smoking, doing drugs and making a ruckus, but they didn't approach or threaten me, as they could clearly see my M-16. Suddenly, several White Mice arrived on their scooters and a jeep to confront these hoodlums. (White Mice was what we called the local police, or maybe they were militia. Regardless of what they actually were, they wore white uniforms and white helmets—hence White Mice.) The teenagers were not fazed and continued to race up and down the street and antagonize the cops. Finally one of them got too close to a cop, who took out his baton and hit the teenager on the side of his head. The kid fell off his scooter, and three White Mice rushed over and beat the crap out of him. I wasn't sure what to do and got out of the guard shack and started to approach the scene when the teenager's friends deserted him and left him to his fate. I didn't know whether they had left to arm themselves and return for a battle, but the White Mice picked up the kid, loaded him into a jeep and left. Sometime later, two teenagers returned, picked up their friend's scooter and sped away.

I went back to the guard shack, fully expecting something else to happen. About an hour later, I heard a loud commotion coming from a block or two away, but whatever was happening stayed there. I heard yelling and the noise of several motorbikes, but no gunshots. These noises went on almost all night, with disturbances happening fairly close to my location. Finally, the ruckus got much louder, and I put the M-16 to my shoulder, wanting to be ready for whatever would happen next. I fully expected these teenagers to try something on the R&R hotel, as they were aware that everyone inside the hotel was dead drunk and couldn't put up any resistance. Not that they were going to launch a full-scale assault, but they probably wanted to mess up the R&R center. All that was between them and the hotel was me.

I quickly took three more full magazines out of one of the bandoliers and placed them on the counter of the guard shack within easy reach and assumed a defensive position. The noise continued until I heard the noise of several motorbikes speeding away from my post. I remained hyper alert in case they turned back, but several minutes of quiet allowed me to relax. Soon, all I could hear were the normal sounds of nighttime (i.e., crickets, night birds and whatever else made noises at night). Finally, after a long, stressful night, I was relieved of my guard duty and passed the assignment to my replacement.

20

The Green Berets
Asked Us to Find a Concealed
.51-Caliber Machine Gun

We had just finished our last infrared target area at the base of Nui Ba Den (the 3,200-foot mountain located near the Cambodian border) and contacted the Green Beret outpost located on the summit of the mountain for artillery clearance out of the area when they asked us to try to locate a .51-caliber machine gun that had been damaging and shooting down their supply helicopters. They gave us several possible coordinates for the machine gun and advised us that they thought the gun was mounted on some sort of carriage and was therefore mobile. It could be moved quickly before gunships and artillery could locate it. I quickly plotted several possible locations for the gun and checked my map for clearings and other openings in the jungle that would allow an anti-aircraft machine gun that fired large bullets a clear view of the mountaintop (and consequently a clear view of approaching helicopters). There were very few clearings, as this area was made up of triple canopy jungle from horizon to horizon.

As we circled the area, the sun was still below the eastern horizon and long shadows filled the jungle below us. We checked out several of the suggested locations for the gun but found the jungle too dense to allow a machine gun to be wheeled into place, fired and then wheeled away. I pointed to a small clearing on my map, just barely visible from the air, as a possible hiding place. We decided that we would dive from 1,000 feet to treetop level and blast over the clearing at maximum power and prop levels to see whether there was any activity at the edge of the clearing. While we were flying around looking at possible sites for the gun, I was listening to AFVN (the armed services radio out of Saigon), and as we dived toward the jungle, the DJ started playing the theme from *For a Few Dollars More*, one of Clint Eastwood's new spaghetti westerns.

An infrared photograph of a village with a foot bridge and a canal with rice paddies.

As the Jew's harps twanged in my ears, we blasted over the clearing, shaking the treetops as we passed over a squad of NVA troops pulling a mobile .51-caliber machine gun out of the jungle. We surprised them, as a Mohawk is very quiet in its approach and very quick for a propeller plane. Our sudden appearances and disappearances usually did not allow any accurate fire to be directed at us.

We quickly called the Nui Ba Den artillery people and gave them the coordinates for the small clearing and the gun. We stayed at treetop level for a little longer and then climbed to a few hundred feet to do a BDA (bomb damage assessment) after the 105 mm artillery guns had done their work. We came around and quickly passed over the clearing, which was still smoldering from the impact of the bombardment. We couldn't see anything because of the smoke and came around again. This time we saw the ruins of a mobile .51-caliber machine gun. We did not see any bodies, so we assumed that they ran back into the jungle after our initial pass over their location.

We reported to the Green Beret artillery commander that the gun had been destroyed. We also asked whether there was anything else that they would like us to investigate, as we had the fuel to make additional passes around the area. They told us that we didn't have to look around because there was the report of only one gun harassing the supply choppers. We felt a sense of satisfaction that no additional helicopters would be lost to that machine gun.

The *For a Few Dollars More* theme song had finished while we were doing our assessment, and it seemed somehow a fitting accompaniment to our mission. We typically listened to several different radios at the same time, so it was nothing out of the ordinary to be listening to AFVN while talking to artillery fire support bases, other airplanes and each other in the cockpit.

A nighttime infrared photograph showing a river recon with a village, grave mounds and bomb craters.

21

Flat Tire and a Ride in a Loach with the 1/9th Cavalry Scout Platoon

Major Taylor and I were on a daytime photo/VR mission in the area near Phuoc Vinh, the new 1st Cavalry Division headquarters. We needed to land at Phuoc Vinh so that Major Taylor could complete some paperwork regarding needed troop replacements. As we touched down on the runway and reversed the propellers and applied the brakes, we ran over some sharp debris on the runway and punctured our left main landing gear tire. Major Taylor and I had developed a knack for having something happen to our landing gear. Either the gear would not come down properly, so that we would have to bounce the airplane around to get the gear to lock into place, or we would blow out a tire in the boonies.

Phuoc Vinh was a helicopter airfield, and there was not a Mohawk tire close to our location. We were stuck there for the rest of the day and were told that a new tire would not arrive by helicopter until the next morning.

The major went about filling out his replacement requests, and I walked around the base, looking at the different types of helicopters. There were huge numbers of Hueys parked and landing and taking off. There were also Cobra gunships and small helicopters called Loaches that were used for scouting missions. I came to a group of helicopters that belonged to the 1/9th Cavalry. There were Huey slicks (infantry-carrying helicopters), Huey hogs or gunships, Cobras and Loaches. The 1/9th was the scout company for the 1st Cavalry and was composed of white teams (Loaches for scouting), while red teams used the Huey gunships and the Cobras, and blue teams used Huey lift ships for the infantry quick-response teams. As I passed one of the Loaches, a young warrant officer jumped out of the cockpit and asked me, after he saw my Nomex fire-retardant flight suit, if I was one of the Mohawk guys. I replied that I was, and he asked whether I had ever been on a scout mission in a Loach. I told him that I hadn't, and he asked if I wanted to go on one. I said, "Sure, but let me get the OK from the major."

I found Major Taylor and told him that I had been invited to go on a scout mission in a Loach, and if it was OK with him, I would like to go. He said, "OK, just don't get yourself killed; we have some important missions to fly tomorrow." I got my flight helmet and went back to the Loach and said, "It's OK with the major; let's go." The warrant officer pilot said, "Where is your weapon?" I patted my .38 in its holster, and he said, "No, no, no, let's get you a real gun," and he took me to a supply tent where he told the sergeant to loan me an M-16 with several bandoliers of ammunition, multiple hand grenades and several different-colored smoke grenades. He also got me a flak vest to wear, and off we went to his helicopter.

The Loach was a small helicopter that could hold four people; it was fast and extremely maneuverable. The pilot asked me whether I had ever done low-level flying, and I just looked at him and said, "Are you kidding me? How does fifty to seventy-five feet off the ground sound to you, with the power and prop levers near max in a twin-engine fixed-wing aircraft?" He grinned and said, "You haven't seen low-level flying yet the way that we do it." We walked to his helicopter, and I assisted as best I could with his preflight check. When all looked good, we climbed in, and I sat in the left seat versus the right (where I normally sat in the Mohawk). This Loach was equipped with a miniature gun that could be used for defense or offence when needed.

We lifted off, and the pilot told me we were going to check out some trails known to be frequently used by NVA soldiers coming into Vietnam from Cambodia. The trails were located a few miles from Phuoc Vinh, and several of them led off in different directions, most heading for Cambodia. The trick to trail surveillance missions with a Loach was to hover directly over the trail, close enough to the ground to count footprints. We hovered about ten feet off the ground and moved slowly forward, trying to see fresh footprints on the trail. While we did this, we had to constantly look forward, side to side and behind us in case someone popped up from a spider hole with an RPG or even an AK-47, which could have done a great deal of damage to us at that close range. Most of the Loach scout missions were conducted with Huey or Cobra gunships flying cover for the scout. These missions were called pink teams (scouts were white teams and gunships were red teams—hence pink). If the scout ship found anything or got into trouble, the gunships were overhead to jump to the rescue, and if things got out of hand, the blue infantry teams were brought in to assist.

We followed trails for several hundred feet—long enough to determine whether the trails had been used recently—and did not find any evidence of usage. We then switched from trail recon to field and clearing recon, but again we did not encounter any resistance. At all times during our mission, the pilot advised me to fire at any movement that I saw on the ground or in the bushes, as there were no friendlies in our mission area. Several times I saw bushes move and strained my eyes to find the source of the movement, only to discover that the downforce from the rotor blades had caused the movement. We flew around for about two hours without discovering any evidence of the enemy using the trails or clearings. We spoke with other scout ships in the general area, but everyone reported negative contact and didn't see any indication of recent trail usage. We returned to base and did a postflight check of the helicopter, found no damage or fluid leaks, and completed the flight logbook.

I thanked my warrant officer friend for the ride and asked whether he wanted to look at our Mohawk. He said "sure," so we headed for my airplane. I released the telescoping cockpit step and opened my hatch. I gave him a thorough briefing on the airplane, showing him my infrared system controls; then he climbed into the pilot's seat and gazed at the instruments, shaking his head in appreciation. After we finished, he left and I headed out to find food and a place to spend the night.

Early the next morning, a Huey arrived with our new tire and wheel, and crew chiefs jacked up the plane and changed out the damaged tire and wheel for the new one. We taxied to the runway, gained altitude and headed for our assigned photo/VR missions.

22

Black Knight 22,
You Have Two Bogeys
Approaching from the Rear

Nui Ba Den, the 3,200-foot mountain near the Cambodian border, was to our right rear as we headed for our next infrared target area. It was a moonless night and exceedingly dark outside our aircraft. The jungle was 800 feet below us and extended in all directions to the horizon. I studied my map again to find any features that could assist us in navigation, but there was nothing—no roads, no streams or small rivers, no villages, no small hills, just miles and miles of triple canopy trackless jungle. Not a good place to parachute into in case something happened to the airplane. We had to rely on our Doppler navigation system to tell us where the next target area was located.

We arrived at the alleged start of our runs, and I turned on the system and watched the TDIs (terrain display indicators) for any hot spots or cold spots that would indicate human presence. Hot spots would indicate small fires not visible from the air, while cold spots could indicate parked vehicles. However, vehicles in this area would be an impossibility because there were no roads and the jungle was too thick. Human beings could only get around on their own two feet or maybe on the back of an elephant. I looked at my pilot, Mr. Williams, with whom I had flown countless missions, and said, "This is hopeless and a waste of time; we cannot get any readings through this thick jungle."

We continued flying at a lower altitude, thinking that if there was something below us, being closer to the ground would allow the infrared system to detect it. There continued to be nothing but darkness, and then our Doppler navigation failed along with much of our other electronics. The compass still worked, of course, as did our radios, and the instruments were operational, including my infrared system, but other than that, we were lost. With no landmarks visible, my map was useless too. We circled for a couple of minutes to try to get our bearings when suddenly we both noticed a very faint light in the distance. It flickered on and off as the tree branches hid it, and we decided to head for it to see whether we could regain our bearings. The light had to be from a village; all we had to do was fly to it, and I would locate it on my map, and then we would fly a compass heading back to where we knew where we were.

It was still pitch black as we headed toward that flickering light with our navigation lights illuminated. As we got closer and closer, I studied my map to try to predetermine the location of that light. We were still flying at about 500 feet, and as we approached the light, an airfield emerged from the jungle, and suddenly runway lights came on as we flew directly over the runway; my equipment picked up two hot spots on top of two cold spots. Mr. Williams and I both looked down and saw, to our dismay, two Migs (bogeys) moving on the taxiway headed for the runway. We had flown directly to and over an NVA airstrip hidden in the Cambodian jungle. We now knew exactly where we were (well, we kind of knew where we were) and took a compass heading back toward Vietnam. We didn't care where we entered Vietnam airspace— we just needed to get that accomplished as quickly as possible before we became air-to-air missile fodder. Our two turboprop engines put out a lot of heat, and a missile would have no trouble at all locking onto that heat signature.

We knew that the trees in this whole area were about 100 feet tall and immediately headed for them as we extinguished our navigation lights. I kept looking back at the airfield to see whether the Migs had gotten airborne, but we were too low now and I could not see anything. We put that Mohawk onto the treetops and hoped that no tree had grown higher than the ones around it. We were sure that by now the Migs were airborne and had started to hunt for us. We also realized that because they were so much faster than us, they would need to slow down to try to get a fix on us and not overshoot and miss us they sought to get a missile lock-on. I don't know whether these Mig models carried guns too or just missiles. If they did have guns, they really didn't have to acquire a positive lock onto us; they could fire in our general direction and hope for a hit.

Many times we heard a tone in our headsets that indicated a brief lock-on, but the heavy foliage and our treetop altitude prevented a sustained lock-on. Because the Migs were so fast, they had to swing back and forth behind us or do a tight 360 to try to get a better missile lock. They evidently had done a 360-degree turn, seeking to get a better angle behind us, and, in so doing, attracted the attention of our radar net people.

We heard a call over one of our radios: "Unidentified aircraft approaching Vietnam airspace on a heading of such and such, identify yourself." We immediately responded to the radar net people, who needed us to squawk a specific frequency that would positively identify us an American aircraft. We were still a ways from Vietnam when the radar net people alerted us to two bogeys approaching us rapidly from the rear. We acknowledged that we knew we were being chased, and the radar guys were kind enough to remind us every few seconds that the bogeys were gaining on us. "Hey, radar guys, we know that they are there—we can feel their hot breath breathing on our necks." (We didn't really say that, but that is what we felt.) The radar guys next told us that two Fox 4s (Phantoms) had been scrambled from Bien Hoa to intercept us.

At this point in time, dawn was starting to break, but the sun was still well below the horizon. The radar guys continued to update us about the bogeys, which had slowed to try to get a visual of us, but the color of the Mohawk, our treetop altitude and the jungle vegetation kept us camouflaged, and only occasionally would we hear a lock-on tone in our headsets that would just as quickly fade away. Out in front of us, we started to be able to see some faint ground features, and then in the sky, coming directly toward us, we could see the exhaust trails of the two Phantoms as they arrived with afterburners blazing (which created the exhaust trails). Our radio crackled, and the lead jet pilot came on and asked us to flash our landing light so that they could positively identify us and not launch a missile or two at us instead of the Migs. We flashed our light, and shortly after that, two Phantoms shot past us, one on our right and one on our left at the same altitude as us. We looked at each other and said, "Holy shit, how did we escape that situation?"

A few seconds later, the radar net people contacted us and advised us that the Migs had turned tail as soon as their radar alerted them to the inbound Phantoms. A couple of minutes later, our two Phantoms came up to us, one on each side again, with their gear and flaps down to stay with us for a few seconds. All four crew members waved at us and gave us the thumbs-up sign; then the gear came up and the flaps were repositioned, and they thundered away toward the rising sun. We, of course, thanked them for coming to rescue us and thanked the radar net people for scrambling the Phantoms to our heading. We then headed for home, as fuel was going to become an issue if we had to do any additional evasive maneuvers.

23

Cats Supposedly Have Nine Lives, How Many Do People Have?

I Used Six or More of Mine on One Mission

I was starting to be a "short-timer," meaning that I had about thirty days or less to serve in Vietnam. I had flown more than 1,000 hours of combat assault missions, and this night I had been chosen to fly with a captain who was new in-country. This officer was, unfortunately for me, one of the few who were "know-it-alls." I was assigned to fly an infrared mission near Nui Ba Den, the 3,200-foot mountain that rose out of the surrounding jungle near the Cambodian border. The mountain was very heavily forested and the only obstruction to aircraft in that part of Vietnam. The top of the mountain was controlled by a Green Beret outpost, and the remainder of the mountain and the land around the base was controlled by the NVA. Our mission that night was to fly several infrared target areas to find clusters of enemy troops and possibly trace their trails back to the Cambodian border. The night was clear and great for flying, as Nui Ba Den did not have any lights on the summit to aid in navigation to prevent someone from flying into the mountainside.

The new captain was "all Army," meaning that every word out of my mouth was supposed to be preceded by "Sir" and end with "Sir." That was a short-lived expectation on his part. He was a joy; he had no personality, was rude and obnoxious, and knew everything about Vietnam even though he had been in-country for only a couple of weeks. We spoke at our briefing table, and I asked him if he was familiar with our target area and if he knew how to get there and return to base. He replied, "Of course I know the area; I flew there with our check pilot during the day a few days ago." I then said, "You haven't been in that area at night?" He replied, "No, is there a problem with that?" "Yes," I replied, "there is a 3,200-foot mountain called Nui Ba Den in the middle of our target area that is constantly being bombarded with rockets, mortars and heavy machine-gun fire—specifically .51-caliber machine guns. The mountain slopes are difficult to see at night, and we have to be cognizant of our location at all times: we have to completely trust our Doppler navigation equipment." I could see from his body language that he was not putting much value in what I was telling him. After all, what could an E-5 with over 11 months in-country possibly know that a captain didn't know better? At that point, another experienced captain said to my pilot, "Listen to what he is telling you about that area, as he and I have been out there many times and he knows what he is talking about; what he says may save your life." My pilot looked at the other pilot, then at me, and said, "Let's go." All I could do is look at the other captain and shake my head; he returned my emotion and mouthed "Good luck."

We proceeded to the flight line and performed a preflight inspection of the aircraft and found all to be in order. After the engines had started, I performed the system check on my infrared equipment, and it, too, checked out fine. We taxied toward the end of the runway and called out, "Hot and locked," meaning that the ejection seats were now armed and the side canopies were locked in the closed position, ready for takeoff. We were cleared for takeoff and rolled down the runway, picking up speed—a little slower than normal, I thought, but we were moving fairly quickly when I heard through my headset, "BLACK KNIGHT 24, ABORT TAKEOFF, ABORT TAKEOFF, ABORT TAKEOFF, YOU ARE ON FIRE."

We had nearly reached rotation speed to get airborne when the tower told us to abort our takeoff. My pilot immediately slammed the plane back onto the runway, reversed the propellers and stood on the brakes. The plane shuddered like it was coming apart and stopped. Before I could open my hatch, the plane was surrounded by firefighting ground crew personnel. I looked at my pilot. "What is going on?" he screamed. "We are on fire!" The left main landing gear tire had started to seize and the overheated tire and brake assembly caught fire, and the fire started to climb up the strut toward a fuel tank. The pilot looked at me and asked, "Didn't you hear the tower tell us to abort because of a fire?" I said "Yes, I did, but you have control of the airplane, not me, and I fully expected you to handle the situation."

At this time, the fire crew was trying to pull me out of the burning airplane while others were trying to put out the fire. I yelled at them to wait a second while I disarmed my ejection seat and then grabbed the pilot by the arm and yelled at him to disarm his seat. He had forgotten to disarm his seat, and had it gone off in the cockpit while on the ground, several of us would have been killed. He disarmed his seat while I removed the seat leg straps from my calves. These straps, in the event of ejecting, pull your legs back tightly against the front bottom edge of the ejection seat. This prevents your legs from flying up and smashing on the top cockpit frame as you go through the top canopy. If not for the straps, you would have both of your legs broken or worse as you exited the plane. With the straps off our legs, both of us dove out of the cockpit into the arms of the fire crew, who quickly pulled us away from the burning airplane. The fire crew quickly extinguished the fire, and we watched as the airplane was pulled off the active runway and to a safe spot on a taxiway. That was life number one and perhaps number two if I had not noticed the pilot's still-armed ejection seat.

We were driven back to the flight line and assigned another airplane. The captain did not talk about our close call, which I thought was strange, as I think that most people would talk about the experience and how lucky we were to get back onto the runway instead of having to deal with an airplane on fire at that low altitude. We did our preflight checks and, without any other problems, were given clearance to leave. We took off toward the ocean and circled back directly over the Vung Tau lighthouse, and I cleared the Doppler navigation system to reflect our current location over the lighthouse.

After clearing the Vung Tau airspace, I contacted Nui Dat artillery and requested a clear flight path up the corridor from Victor Tango (Vung Tau) to Bravo Hotel (Bien Hoa). Nui Dat was manned by an Australian artillery company, and it was always fun to listen to their accents as they told us of any outgoing fire missions that would affect our line of flight. After Bien Hoa, we would have to contact Cu Chi artillery for clearance past them and into no man's land.

As we approached our first target area near the base of Nui Ba Den, we could see explosions on the mountainside and at the top as both sides lobbed artillery shells and rockets and mortars at each other, accompanied by streams of red and green tracers from machine guns and small-arms fire. My pilot was mesmerized by the fireworks, and I had to get his attention so that we could fly our target area. He checked the Doppler and lined us up for our first run. We completed that area and moved to the next area while dodging tracer fire directed at us. They could not see us but shot at the engine noise.

As we turned toward our next target area, I pointed out a spectacle in front of us: a "Puff the Magic Dragon" C-47 gunship that was equipped with mini guns inside the fuselage that could fire streams of bullets, which at night looked like a stream of red from a fire hose. Puff was working an area closer to the base of the mountain and making wide circles, as the plane had to be tilted for the mini guns to be aimed at the ground. We would be working an area that was bordering on the edge of the area Puff was working, although we would not be in any danger of overlapping as long as we paid attention to where we were. We had finished three passes of eight and were turning for pass number four. I pointed out that Puff was working to our right and above us and that we should turn well before we got anywhere hear him. We were moving along nicely when we started to receive a lot of ground fire. I turned from my equipment to monitor the incoming .51-caliber tracers that had started to track us. Puff noticed the tracers and directed some of his attention toward the machine gun, and it was soon silenced. I advised the captain of the situation regarding the tracers, and he acknowledged my report. I then told him that, according to our Doppler equipment, we should be nearing our present run's termination.

Suddenly green tracers raced past my side of the airplane, and I glanced at two things at once. The first was the Doppler readout—we were past our turnaround point—and the second was Puff, fast approaching us with his red fire hose of tracers. With our current heading, we would pass directly under and into his mini gun stream of fire. I yelled at the captain to turn left, hard left, and dive as I pointed at Puff with mini guns fully ablaze. We went right wing over and dove toward the ground and away from Puff. Life number three passed through me....

We both were pretty shaken up by our near-death experience and flew around in a clear airspace area for a few minutes until our respiration rate had slowed significantly. We had to stay clear of our next target area, as Puff was still operating and the incoming and outgoing artillery fire and machine-gun fire was intense. After about an hour of flying in circles and dodging incoming small-arms and machine-gun fire, we were able to approach our next target area, which thankfully was away from all the action. We made our runs with the infrared system working flawlessly. That area was quiet and the system did not display anything at all. It was just a huge expanse of quiet triple canopy jungle.

During the time that we were running our mosaic of the target area, the pilot was very quiet. Usually, there would be conversation in the cockpit about what had happened or what was going on around us on the ground, especially with all the activity we had witnessed. Anyone else I flew with would have been talking about Puff and the damage that C-47 could do to troops on the ground, or something related to the mission and the fact that our recent target areas were so quiet. The captain kept his thoughts to himself, so I ignored him and concentrated on my equipment, ready to react to anything I saw. Usually when I flew with someone who didn't fly in I Corps, he had lots of questions about the differences between flying there and here and whether there had been any interesting missions. This guy evidently could not care less, and I didn't care either.

We had one more target area to map and proceeded to that location. This area proved to be quiet as well, and we ran our runs and completed our mosaic of the area. This target area was the same as the previous one, with nothing of interest anywhere. There were no trails, roads, streams, or hills—nothing except miles of thick jungle. Normally, with a regular pilot, we would discuss why we weren't picking up anything in the area and joke that the NVA must have packed up and gone home, or else they were all already in Saigon or Vung Tau.

With our target areas completed, we started to head for home but had to detour around a large firefight that was being supported by artillery, helicopter gunships and fast movers (Air Force and Navy jets). We had finally cleared the area when the captain asked me how long it would take to get back to Vung Tau to land. I told him that normally it would take just under an hour to get back. He then looked at me and said, "With all the maneuvers and detours we experienced, we don't have enough fuel to make it back to Vung Tau. We need to look for a place to set down and refuel." There were several fire support bases with runways that we could use, but all of them were taking heavy incoming rocket and mortar fire. We then headed for the 1st Cavalry quarters located at Phuoc Vinh and requested clearance to land and refuel.

The area was quiet as we approached the runway and set down, but we were told that the POL dump for refueling was at the opposite end of the runway from where we were, and we would have to make a U-turn and taxi back to the refueling point. We did that and pulled off the active runway to a paved area where the fuel bladders and trucks were located. We had just arrived and were preparing to shut down as a fuel truck with JP-4 started to move toward us when the truck stopped, turned into a revetment area, and shut down. We watched as the driver and another guy jumped from the truck and ran for a bunker. We were still wearing our helmets and could not hear what was going on outside the airplane, with the engine noise blocking out noises. Then we saw the explosions and understood that the camp was under heavy attack by rockets and mortars. The incoming munitions did not appear to be targeting any specific area, instead randomly exploding all over the camp. We needed to move, as we did not want to be anywhere near the POL depot if a rocket got lucky and scored a direct hit on the fuel dump.

We taxied back onto the active runway, and the tower gave us clearance to immediately take off. We started to roll and gained speed quickly, and as we moved down the runway, we could see many explosions on both sides of the runway. The camp was taking a beating, and we wanted to get our butts out of there as quickly as we could. We were just about to lift off when the tower screamed for us to abort our takeoff. For the second time that night, we slammed back down onto the runway, pulled maximum propeller reversal and stood on the brakes. We had just touched back down on the runway with the propellers reversed when a number of Cobra and Huey gunships roared by, just over our heads and in front of us down the runway. If the tower had not told us to abort, we would have lifted off into the middle of the helicopter flight, which had been scrambled to hunt down the rocket and mortar locations. We thanked the guys in the tower, who told us to leave again because they were heading for a bunker.

We taxied very quickly to the end of the runway, spun around and, with the power and prop levers at max, hustled down the runway. Explosions were still constantly going off on both sides, and then the runway in front of us exploded in flames and smoke. The captain pulled back on the stick, and because we were light on fuel, the airplane wanted to fly quicker than usual. As he pulled back on the stick and kept his right hand on the power levers, I reached over and pushed the landing gear lever forward to retract the gear. We roared through those flames and smoke, with debris bouncing off the wings and fuselage. Keep in mind that the reason we were there in the first place was because we needed to refuel, and now we had just experienced two takeoff attempts to get our butts out of that place. Lives four and five (and probably more) streaked past me....

After lifting off from Phuoc Vinh, we headed for Bien Hoa, but because of the activity all around the area, we couldn't get clearance to land. Air Force jets had the place monopolized, and all we could do was bypass the airport and head for Vung Tau. The captain pulled back on the power levers to conserve as much fuel as possible when a red warning light glowed, indicating a low fuel supply. He asked me how much flying time we had after the light went on, and I responded, "I'm sorry, but I don't know because in 1,000 hours of flying I never experienced this situation." I repeated that I truly was sorry that I didn't know the answer to his question. He reached for the dials of one of our radios and contacted another Mohawk pilot from Vung Tau and was told that when the red low-fuel light went on, there was about ten minutes of flight time left. Unfortunately, we were still twelve to fifteen minutes away from the runway! He looked at me and told me that he was going to gain some altitude in case we had to eject—that would give the ejection seats additional time and altitude to properly deploy their parachutes. If we did have to eject in the next few minutes, we would probably land in the Saigon River, fairly close to land, but a lot would depend on our altitude when ejecting and the strength and direction of the wind. We of course would send out a mayday call just prior to ejecting with our location speed and heading, which would cause a rescue helicopter to scramble.

We could see the runway lights in the distance, and the captain called the tower and reported a critical low fuel emergency. We were cleared for a direct approach, and the crash trucks were scrambled into position. As we slowly approached the runway, I stared out of my hatch window at the spinning propeller blades that were mere feet from my face and willed them to keep spinning. We stayed at a much higher altitude for landing than normal, just in case the engines died, as we needed height for the seats to have time to work properly without killing us (for example, you could not eject from the airplane while it was still on the ground). The power levers were pulled back slightly, the flaps deployed, and finally the gear was lowered. We hit the runway, and as the captain reversed the propellers, nothing happened—they just spun with no sound. He applied the brakes, and we coasted to a stop with the crash trucks on either side of us. Life number six (at least) knocked on my hatch window as I said, "Cold and unlocked," to the captain, who replied, "Cold and unlocked."

As we were driven back to the debriefing area, the captain did not say a word to me. We both were asked questions about the mission and the low fuel situation. I replied that we had tried to refuel at several locations, but due to the level of enemy activity at each location, we either could not land or, when we did, were told to immediately depart. I mentioned that we were nearly destroyed at Phuoc Vinh during takeoff by rockets making direct hits on the runway, but the captain was able to get the airplane airborne and out of harm's way. The captain was questioned about the low fuel situation, but with our reports and the fact that everyone flying that night in that general area reported the enemy activity, the questions stopped and we were told that we were lucky we had made it home and landed safely.

The colonel took me aside after our debriefing and after the captain had left for his hotel and bar and asked me to tell him about the entire mission, from the fire during our initial takeoff until we landed with no fuel. The colonel knew me and recognized my extensive flight time both in I Corps and in III Corps and could easily tell that I was still pissed off by the captain's handling of the entire mission. We sat and talked, and I described what had happened that night, but I also gave credit to the captain for becoming cool headed toward the end of the mission when the low-fuel light came on. I repeated that the captain had tried to land at least twice to refuel, but we were not cleared to land. I then looked at the colonel and said, "I never want to be assigned to fly with him again." The colonel nodded and told me I could go and that he was glad things had turned out the way that they did. I nodded and left.

I never flew with that captain again, and I was told that he dramatically cut down his flying hours. He did volunteer for a job that required only a minimum number of flight-time hours per month to continue to receive flight pay.

These were several different times during that mission when I was able to look back and say, "What if?"

24

UFO and Something Else

We were returning from a mission outside of Cu Chi and fairly close to the Cambodian border at about 4:00 a.m. when the radar net people contacted us about an unidentified bogey that was in front of us at about the same altitude. The object was clearly visible on the radar screen, and we were told to take immediate evasive action to avoid a midair collision. We did as instructed and were told that the object would not respond to air traffic control. As we took evasive action, the radar net people warned us that the object had also turned and was approaching us from the rear. We again took evasive action, but the object stayed with us as we turned left, swerved right, climbed and dove; the thing followed our every move. As this was happening at 4:00 a.m., the radar people had alerted 1st Cavalry units on the ground to this unidentified threat, and the closest unit launched, call sign "Blue Max" Cobra gunships, to assist us in driving off the object or destroying it if it attacked us or them.

No matter what we did, the object stayed with us and several times closed to near-collision distances. This entire situation was not going well because the radar guys were getting nervous that whatever this thing was, it might break off from us and head for the U.S. Army command center in Saigon. Those on the Blue Max Cobra gunships were anxious to see something, and I could imagine them buzzing around us with their fingers on the triggers. I fully expected us to become a large fireball in the sky because of the way the object flew around us. At one point, it came to a halt, and we were directed to fly directly over it with our infrared system turned on to see whether it would show up on my equipment. However, nothing appeared on my TDI (terrain display indicator) screens. Since it was still nighttime and pitch black outside our cockpit, we could not see anything except the navigational lights on the Cobra gunships that hovered and buzzed around below us.

Once again, the object headed directly toward us at the same altitude, and we braced for the midair collision as the radar net guys told us that the thing was still on a collision course with us and closing quickly. We waited, fully expecting to see gunfire or hear missile lock-on directed at us. Both of us cinched up our parachute harnesses and waited for the inevitable explosion—maybe we would be lucky and just lose a wing or suffer a damaged tail stabilizer—and as the radar net guys counted down the time and distance to impact, we stared out the cockpit windscreen to catch a glimpse of our tormenter. The time ran out, and nothing happened; the radar net guys urgently called our call sign and announced that the object, after apparently colliding with us, had disappeared from radar. They asked us to circle for a few minutes in case it returned, but after fifteen or twenty minutes of circling the area, we were cleared to depart for home.

None of us that night ever saw anything, but whatever the object was, it had clearly showed up on the radar screens. We had been chasing and were chased by *something* for an hour, and we were tired and totally wired as we strained our ears for another radar contact alert, but all stayed quiet as we headed for Vung Tau. We spoke about what had happened and speculated about what the object was or could have been. Was it a super-secret U.S. spy plane that could fool radar? Was it a Chinese or Soviet craft that was being tested, or was it something else entirely? We never found out.

After this incident, I thought about another unexplained situation that I had experienced a few years earlier when I was in high school. It was mid–November and late afternoon when I returned home from school and decided that since I still had a couple hours of light left and it was still upland bird hunting season, I would head out into the woods and try to stir up a partridge. It was a cold day with heavy clouds as I headed out the door with my trusty old Ithaca 20-gauge double-barreled shotgun. The woods where I was heading were 500 acres owned by my grandparents and comprised the typical New England collection of hardwoods, pine, hemlock and spruce, with many clumps of thick mountain laurel. I knew the land well, as I had traveled these woods since I could walk, and headed for a hillside that sloped for about a mile down to a small lake or large pond.

I was on the hillside about a mile from home and was passing close to an incredibly thick stand of hemlock trees and mountain laurel bushes when the thicket next to me exploded. If you have ever been close to a partridge when it gets startled and blasts away from you, you will know what I mean when I say it exploded out of the thicket and zigzagged away from me through the hardwood trees. You would swear that a herd of elephants had just left that thicket with all the noise that bird generated. Partridges generally do not fly very far after being disturbed; I saw another hemlock and mountain laurel thicket about a hundred feet in front of me, and I was sure that the bird had landed there. I realized that my chances of getting a shot at the bird were nonexistent, but the thrill of the chase was in my blood.

I approached the new thicket from the uphill side and discovered that this thicket was huge in comparison to the one that had held the bird. The thicket was about seventy-five feet long and forty to fifty feet across, and it was in a depression that was about one to two feet deep. The thicket was heavily covered with eight- to ten-foot-tall hemlock and spruce trees that grew so thickly together that you could not see more than a foot in any direction. I paused at the top edge of the thicket and listened for any evidence that the partridge was within, but all I could hear was the light wind blowing through the hardwood trees, causing the remaining dead leaves to rattle against their branches, and the pines and hemlocks whistled slightly as the wind blew through the needles.

I was convinced that the bird was in the thicket and was determined to flush it out, just to hear it take off. I stepped down into the thicket depression and took a step forward, but I immediately stopped, as I could not see beyond a foot in front of my face. I used the barrel of my shotgun to move some branches, and as I did, every hair on the back of my neck stood at attention. I stopped and carefully looked around and listened; there was no sound, no gentle wind blowing the dead leaves or pine needles—everything was absolutely quiet. I took half a step forward, and something told me to stop and back up out of there. I slowly backed up while straining my eyes and ears to hear or see something. I retreated out of the depression, and suddenly the breeze began to blow again, the dead leaves rattled against their branches, small winter birds chirped, crows cawed and the hair on my neck relaxed. I stood there, looking at the thicket and listening to the noises around me, and said, "This is stupid."

I then walked around the short side of the thicket to the downhill side and walked along the long edge of the thicket for a few paces before turning toward it. I held my shotgun at the ready and stepped down and into the thicket again. This time I advanced two steps before the tree branches closed in around me, and no matter how I tried, using the barrel of my shotgun to move branches aside, I still could not see more than a foot in any direction when my mind screamed, "You are being watched!" I stood still and looked left and right, listening for any sound near me. As I listened, the wind stopped again, the crows stopped cawing, the dead leaves on the trees hung silent, and I felt a presence near me in the thicket. "OK," I said, "time to back out of here again." I slowly moved back to the edge of the depression and carefully stepped out;

then I took another two steps backward and stopped. The wind blew again, the leaves rattled in the trees, the winter birds twittered and the crows resumed making a racket.

I walked around the bottom of the thicket and climbed the hill to look down into it to see whether I could detect any movement, but all was still as the first snowflakes of the approaching storm landed on my face. I stood there for a minute or so trying to understand what I had experienced but decided that some things cannot be explained. I headed for home with about a mile to travel as the snow began to fall in earnest. In New England, a major snowstorm starts out softly but quickly picks up to the point that you experience a whiteout. This is what happened as I made my way home. Many times during my trek through the snow and the increasing darkness I turned around and glanced behind me, but I saw nothing but the falling snow. When I arrived home, I didn't mention my time in the thicket to anyone. I went back into the woods many times after that experience but never ventured anywhere near that thicket and never experienced anything like that situation again.

25

Vertigo, 37 mm Anti-Aircraft Guns, GCA Foul-Up and Trucks in the Michelin Rubber Plantation

Mr. Williams and I were assigned a "walk-in-the-park" infrared mission. All we had to do was fly to the Cambodian border near the Parrot's Beak area and run long, straight lines near the border while operating the infrared equipment. No problem, as they probably wouldn't shoot at us from inside Cambodia, and if they shot at us from the Vietnam side, we could clobber them with artillery, gunships, jets or B-52s. All we had to do was sit in the cockpit and look to our right at all the bright lights on the Cambodian side of the border. We would make a few passes, check for any activity below us, and then mosey on to something more interesting. OK!

There were some clouds moving in as we started our rollout down the runway, heading into the wind toward the ocean, and as we climbed, we were enveloped in very thick clouds. I immediately got vertigo—the first time in nearly a year of flying in all kinds of weather. I told Mr. Williams, and he replied that he, too, had vertigo. I was absolutely positive that we were in a vertical dive to the left and started to reach for the ejection seat handle when Mr. Williams told me that he thought we were in a near vertical climb. We looked at each other and then at the instruments, which indicated that we were in a wing-level flight and climbing normally. We both said, "Keep looking at the instruments, keep looking at the instruments, trust the instruments." After what seemed like an eternity (really only a couple of minutes), we suddenly popped out of the clouds and into a clear, star-filled sky with thick clouds below us. We circled back over the lighthouse, whose beacon we could see reflected in the clouds, and reset the Doppler. Neither one of us, in all the flying we had done together or with other people, had ever experienced vertigo during a flight.

Our flight to the Cambodian border was quiet, but we could see a large firefight happening near the Michelin Rubber Plantation and we avoided that area, as there were numerous airplanes, helicopters and artillery providing support to the 1st Cavalry guys on the ground. Saigon was ahead of us and on the left. It was a large, sprawling city that was lit up well at night, a far cry from the hamlets and villages we saw or smelled as we flew over them in I Corps. Ahead of us was Cu Chi, which (unknown to us at the time) was the home of a massive tunnel system used by the VC and NVA troops. Cu Chi was also a good-sized city that we used as a landmark in bad weather.

As we approached the Cambodian border, we both were amazed at what we saw on the ground in front of us. Across the border, it looked like some sort of festival in the jungle, with multiple lights visible. As we flew very close to the border, we noticed sporadic small-arms fire directed at us as tracers arced up toward the plane. According to protocol, because of the air traffic in this area at night, we had to run with our navigation lights on, which meant that the light on our belly was on as well as our wingtip lights and our tail light. We were just a pretty sitting duck with those lights on. We couldn't believe the activity we were witnessing across the border in Cambodia. "How can this much be going on and we cannot do anything about it?" we asked.

Both of us were leaning forward in our seats, looking at the display below us and slightly to the right, when five flaming basketballs nearly took our nose off. They were so close that they illuminated the entire cockpit as they screamed upward, just missing us. I quickly looked down and right as five more of those flaming basketballs came at us. Mr. Williams had already reacted and had us with a right wing up and over as the second group of 37 mm rounds passed by us in the exact location that our wing had just occupied. We were now in a vertical dive to the left as five more flaming rounds just missed our tail. We had another five to contend with as we dived and pulled away from the border, and they passed behind and above us. A radar-controlled 37 mm anti-aircraft battery on the Cambodian side of the border had locked onto us, and because we had a headwind, the tracking was just off; otherwise they would have blown the entire cockpit off the plane.

During our violent evasive maneuvers, Mr. Williams had turned off our navigation lights and we went treetop level in the dark—again! He then, after we were clear of the danger, got on the radio and reported the event, including the coordinates that I had noted for the battery. The reply was "Sorry, nothing we can do about it, as it came from inside Cambodia, but we are glad you are OK." We didn't say much because Mr. Williams and I had experienced quite a bit of danger together in I Corps when he was new in-country, but this was different: in I Corps, we could do something about an attack like that, but here, because of borders and politics, we couldn't do a thing! We headed for home and asked about the weather because we did not want to experience vertigo again, especially on short final. We were told that the cloud cover had cleared, and we had smooth sailing all the way to the airfield.

Another day, we were on a daytime VR mission, flying toward the Parrot's Beak area along the Cambodian border and approaching Cu Chi. There were several other aircraft in the area heading in the same general direction as us, and I noticed a pair of Cobra gunships ahead of us. They were flying in a trail formation about three hundred feet below our location. I watched them and commented on how narrow the fuselage was when a sudden movement caught my eye: the trailing Cobra abruptly shook, and as I watched, the rotor blades flew off the helicopter. "Holy shit!" I yelled. "They just lost their rotor blades!" We were now ahead of the Cobras, and all I could see was that narrow fuselage spin for a few seconds and then plunge nose first toward the earth. We continued forward, and the helicopter disappeared from view behind us. I didn't want to see the crash anyway.

I understand that there is a critical nut on top of the helicopter mast that secures the rotor blades in place. The unofficial name for this nut is the Jesus nut—aptly named, because if this nut fails at any time, the helicopter immediately loses its rotor blades. Every helicopter pilot and crew chief religiously checks this critical nut during the preflight check, but this particular nut failed for some unknown reason. I didn't see or hear about any incoming ground fire that could have damaged the nut, and the helicopter was not flying erratically in a way that could have stressed the nut. The only logical conclusion was that the nut must have developed a stress crack that was not visible, and it finally failed in flight. Everyone could speculate endlessly about what caused the nut to fail, but the outcome will always be the same. I was shocked as I spoke with Mr. Williams, as neither one of us, in all the hours we had flown, had ever seen another plane or helicopter go down. I didn't want to imagine what those two pilots experienced as they went down, helpless to anything about the crash and their impending deaths. At least in a Mohawk, we had ejection seats if something went wrong and could glide (yeah, right, glide like a brick) and try to land.

We were returning from a daytime mission, and as we approached Vung Tau, we decided that we should try a GCA (ground-controlled approach) guided landing for practice in case we had to land in fog or low-visibility conditions. Mr. Williams contacted the tower and advised them of our intention to do a GCA practice landing. He contacted the GCA shack, and they locked onto us and started to give us heading information and altitude readings, essentially lining us up with the runway. Everything looked good as they had us adjust our altitude and heading until we could see that something was definitely wrong with our direction. In Vung Tau at the time, there was a service road that passed the end of the runway and continued somewhat parallel to the runway but at a slight angle; it resembled a tight V from the air. The GCA shack was near the end of the runway, and somehow the GCA had identified the service road as the runway.

We continued on the GCA heading given to us, lowering the flaps and extending the landing gear, and waited for the last-minute heading correction that would line us up with the runway again. We waited and waited, and Mr. Williams contacted the GCA and asked them to confirm our heading; they responded that we were on the correct heading and on the glide path for landing. We knew that the GCA shack personnel could see our approach if they went outside, and Mr. Williams requested that they do so to reconfirm our progress. We could see someone emerge from the shack, look in our direction and quickly go back inside. Unable to wait any longer for a heading correction, we made it ourselves on short, short final and touched down on the runway. "GCA, we are on the ground on the runway, not on the service road as you had us directed to land on."

Mr. Williams was not pleased with the GCA's performance; both of us commented that we were glad this was practice, not an actual foul weather landing. As we taxied, the GCA people responded that they had experienced an error in their guidance information to us and that somehow their radar was slightly out of calibration, but it was now correctly adjusted. "Somewhat out of calibration!" Mr. Williams exclaimed. "You had us lined up to land on a road, for crying out loud! What if this had been real in the fog? You wouldn't know your mistake until you saw our fireball; how could your equipment be out of calibration when it is your job to ensure that it is calibrated at all times?" I listened to him vent, as there was nothing I could add to what he said anyway.

While we were coming down, the tower observed the entire incident and was about to advise us to abort our landing when we made our last-minute adjustment. There was an investigation, and it was determined that human error was the cause of the error, not equipment malfunction. Adjustments were immediately made to the personnel manning the GCA shack. We tried another practice run with the GCA a few days later, and their guidance was spot on with heading information, altitude and glide-path information. They had us touch down right on the numbers and in the center of the runway—excellent job!

Mr. Williams and several of the other pilots had an informal bet as to who on landing could keep the plane's nose wheel off the ground for the longest time or distance. This process was fairly simple: land the plane on the two main gear wheels, but keep the stick pulled back, thus keeping the nose of the plane up, and try to roll as far down the runway as possible before the nose wheel would touch down. The only problem was, with the nose up in the air, it was difficult to see where we were going vis-à-vis the runway; therefore, the pilot would lean to the left to see ahead and ask me to keep an eye on the location of the edge of the runway on my side. If we started to drift too far to the right, I would say, "Slightly left," and the pilot would brake a little to move us to the left. A few times with a good headwind, we would almost come to a stop before the nose wheel touched. The contests would continue to see who could set the gear down right on the numbers or who could stop in the shortest amount of time and distance. The TO served as the witness, and we always supported whomever we flew with during these unofficial contests.

I was flying with Captain Johnson, and we were doing a nighttime infrared mission near the Michelin Rubber Plantation when I noticed cold spots appearing on my TDIs (terrain display indicators). I noticed that the cold spots were along a road, one of many that crisscrossed through the rubber trees. I did not see any hot spots, which was strange, and told Captain Johnson about what I was seeing with the equipment. He was skeptical about the cold spots, but I was positive that there was something down there, as I had seen cold spots in the past that turned out to be something of interest. I had flown with him several times in the past and found him to be an egotistical S.O.B. who thought that only officers (especially captains) knew everything. I said, "There are definitely things down there that don't belong there." He countered my assessment by arguing, "That is a rubber plantation, and I am sure that there is discarded equipment all through the trees." I had over 1,000 hours of flying with this infrared system and was confident in what I was seeing, and I told him, "You are right that the rubber plantation probably does have discarded equipment scattered throughout the rubber trees, and yes, I am seeing cold spots indicating debris, but these cold spots are lined up along the roadside, and I am picking up very weak hot spots along with the cold spots." We made another pass over the road, and I pointed out the cold spots along the side of the road in an evenly spaced line. I said, "What could it hurt to drop a couple of rounds on that road?"

He finally agreed that maybe there was something down there but still felt that what I was seeing with my system was discarded debris. After thinking about it for a minute, he contacted the closest fire support base and requested a fire mission at the coordinates I gave him. We circled out of the line of fire and waited for the impact of the shells. The explosions from the impacting shells were very close to the road, and immediately after impact, headlights flashed on as several trucks moved out of hiding and headed west on the plantation roads. Captain Johnson got on the radio to the fire support base and yelled, "We have contact; several vehicles are on the move after your initial volley! They are on the road heading west, coordinates such and such, and moving quickly."

The truck drivers knew not to stay on the rubber plantation roads and headed for jungle trails, where they split up and could drive and hide with their lights out. I checked my map and saw several roads, but I was sure that the trucks would not take any of them because they knew we could track their movements. We pursued them for a while and had the artillery fire a few more volleys into the jungle, but the jungle canopy was too thick for artillery to be effective. We circled in widening arcs, trying to pick up hot spots created by the truck engines and exhausts, but the jungle was too thick and we lost them. The captain finally acknowledged that I knew what I was talking about and said, "Good job." Wow, the supreme compliment! When we landed and debriefed, we were told that a 1st Cavalry blue team would be on the ground at first light to look for damage and any evidence of a planned attack on Saigon or the surrounding bases. We were also told that the Cavalry went on alert after hearing about our truck discovery.

One time Major Taylor and I had landed at Bien Hoa to refuel after spending the day flying around Nui Ba Den and the surrounding countryside. Bien Hoa had extremely long runways, and after we refueled, we taxied to a point about halfway down the runway. We were told to hold short of the active runway, as a jet was going to take off in front of us. We looked to our left and could see a black jet on the active runway, gaining speed as it came closer. As it flashed by in front of us, we were stunned to see it was an SR-71 Blackbird with its afterburners flaming. We watched as it left the runway and did a steep climb out and disappeared. That was an incredible sight, and we still couldn't believe our eyes. We were cleared onto the active runway, and with full power on our rollout, we could only imagine what the SR-71 with the afterburners lit felt like. The SR-71 was used for extreme high-altitude reconnaissance over North Vietnam and other places. The typical altitude of a run was 81,000 feet, above the reach of SAM missiles at the time. The jet was capable of speeds up to 2,193 miles per hour. I could not imagine a camera with the power to take useful photos showing detail from 81,000 feet above the target. We could only guess where this particular bird was headed, but it disappeared from view before we had full clearance for takeoff. WOW!

Mr. Williams and I somehow drew the stupidest nighttime mission imaginable. We were matched with a C model ship that had been outfitted with an underwing-mounted strobe light used for nighttime photo missions. This strobe light was the size and length of a torpedo and had a propeller on its nose that spun in the plane's slipstream and charged the strobe light. It was also noisier than the Mohawk itself. Imagine this: You are a group of VC or NVA troops on the ground at night when suddenly you hear this incredibly loud buzzing that sounds like a 10,000-pound bee flying toward you. Suddenly, there is a bright flash, and the buzzing continues until there is another bright flash. These flashes are so bright that they totally illuminate a football field–size (or larger) area on the ground. It is suddenly full daylight, followed by darkness. The buzzing continues, and every few seconds the brilliant light illuminates the ground. The flash is timed to occur at a regular interval and does not vary its speed or altitude, but continues in a straight line. Doesn't this spectacle present a perfect opportunity for some enterprising VC or NVA group to bag themselves a Mohawk on a strobe-light photo mission?

This strobe-light scenario was something new for me. I had never been on a nighttime photo mission before, and I asked Mr. Williams why we were doing this instead of an infrared mission, which would yield much better results. He simply shook his head and said, "Let's go do this and get it over." Luckily, the area chosen for the strobe-light mission was a very wet delta, and we received little incoming small-arms fire, even if we gave them the greatest target in the war. Prior to the strobe light, night photography was performed with a Mohawk equipped with flare pods that were mounted on the top of the plane or on the wing next to the fuselage. I think that each pod could hold thirty flares. The airplane would line up on its flight path with the camera controls set for the speed and altitude of the plane, which was dictated by the illumination power of the flares used. As the run began, the first flare would be fired from its pod and explode below the airplane, briefly illuminating the ground, at which time the camera would take a picture. This sequence would continue until either the flares ran out or the area of interest was fully photographed. At least this method let the airplane continue quietly on its course until the next flare exploded.

I was standing on the ground waiting to climb into the cockpit after my strobe-light mission when I heard the buzzing noise. I looked up but couldn't see anything except the navigation lights of a Mohawk, but the buzzing noise was so loud that it hurt my ears. Some poor guys had gotten roped into running another strobe-light mission. I stood there and shook my head and asked why anyone would bother when they had this fantastic infrared system that I was about to use.

26

Incoming, and No, Lieutenant, You Cannot Fly Under That Bridge

I had just gotten into bed and was almost asleep after a very long all-night infrared mission on top of a VR mission the day before that had lasted until dark. I was exhausted, hot, hungry and mad at the world after being shot at for the past eighteen hours. I had finally relaxed when I heard CRUMP, CRUMP, CRUMP. "Incoming, incoming!" was shouted by several people near my hooch. I rolled over, put my head under my blanket and yelled to no one in particular, "I'm too tired for this crap; leave me alone," and fell asleep with more explosions going off near my platoon area. I awoke several hours later with a thick coating of dirt and dust on my poncho liner; several rounds had exploded nearby, and the debris and dirt had been blown through the screen and onto me. I got up, shook out the poncho liner and went outside to survey the rocket damage. Fortunately, there was little damage to buildings and no one was hurt.

It was around this time that we said goodbye to Major Taylor. He was scheduled to go home in couple of days, and we wanted to give him a send-off to remember. We invited him and the other pilots to our club for a celebration to show him how much we appreciated his leadership during the past year. He was a gentleman who gave you respect and appreciated your work; I was always ready to fly with him, and I believed that if we ever had a situation while flying, he would bring us home. He was a great guy and would be missed.

One of our crew chiefs who was a little rough around the edges led us in a toast that the major would never forget. The crew chief, who had been tasting whiskey all night, began by saying, "Johnny Taylor, you are one hell of a man and, oh, yeah, a ***** good pilot and officer, we will miss you—here's to you, Johnny!" We all hooted and yelled and congratulated the major on making it through his assignment without a scratch and sincerely wished him the best in life. He walked around the platoon and shook hands with each of us and told us to be careful; then he walked over to get himself a drink. He stood around with us for about two hours, swapping stories and talking about what he was going to do at his new assignment. Finally, he finished his drink and walked back to his jeep and home the next day.

We had another pilot, a captain whom I flew with as often as I could, because he was a great guy, and we developed a flying relationship that made each of us comfortable with the other person. On his last night in-country, he came to our club for drinks and a goodbye celebration, similar to the one for Major Taylor. We talked about his new assignment after Vietnam, and, after considering his reply for a minute, he said to me, "I never told you this, but I am going on a special assignment somewhere in the Middle East, where I will be flying a Mohawk doing something that I can't talk about." I said, "Oh, well, be careful. I assume that there will be less ground fire directed at you, or at least I hope so." He nodded and told me that he had enjoyed flying with me and wished me the best; I replied in turn that I felt the same way and told him to be careful. He said, "Thanks," and waved to the guys and left. He went somewhere, did something for someone and couldn't tell anyone anything!

"Pettis, you have been assigned to fly with the new lieutenant; show him the lay of the land and how to get back home again." I walked into the briefing room and met the new in-country lieutenant. He was the same age as me and full of confidence, and he seemed to be a good guy, not overbearing or obnoxious. He looked at the maps and the areas we were going to fly to, and I noticed that he paid special attention to a spot on the Song Be River. I looked more closely at the area and noticed a bridge over the river leading into a town and wondered.

The day was perfect for flying, with blue skies and large fluffy white clouds scattered here and there. As we taxied and got airborne, we shared small talk about home and, since he was new in-country, what he should look for in the air and on the ground. He looked at me and asked, "Are you going to have me fly somewhere and get lost to see if I can find my way back?" I looked at him and simply said, "Yup."

We flew along the Song Be toward Xuan Loc, and I pointed out the ridge that ran close to the river on the side opposite us. I told him that if he ever was running a nighttime infrared mission, he should not cross the river, as the ridge was about 1,200–1,500 feet high and the IR missions were flown at 800–1,000 feet; therefore, the ridge running parallel to the river would pose a severe danger. He looked out his hatch at the river, which was at least a quarter mile wide at this point, and then at the forested ridge running alongside the river. I also noted that if he ever ran a mission across the river, he should fly along and over the bank of the river because there was a low area between the river and the ridge. He nodded; then he asked whether I wanted to do some low-level flying. "Sure, let's go; where do you want to go?" He dove for some rice paddies and ruffled the surface of the water before turning for the river while looking at me for a reaction. I looked at him and said, "I have over 1,000 hours in these things flying with the best pilots and also with a few of the worst who now fly a desk. I have been low-level treetop more often than you have even thought about it."

He then turned downriver and flew over the middle of the river toward the bridge he had been looking at on the maps in the briefing room. I quickly said, "Don't even think about what you are planning to do." "Why, are you afraid?" he asked. "Fly with me a few times, and you will forget that you have that word in your vocabulary," I countered before adding, "If you want to learn something today, do exactly what I tell you to do." He said, "OK, what do you want me to do?" I said, "First, go left, and then line up parallel to the bridge at the same height above the water as the bridge roadway; then slide closer to the side of the bridge and tell me what you see on the side of the bridge." He did as instructed, and as he flew along the side of the bridge, he told me that he saw fishing lines hanging from the bridge roadway into the water. I said, "Fishing lines? Try thin steel cables that are purposely hung from the bridge to catch the daring helicopter pilots that want to impress everyone on board with their bravado and low-level flying skills. Those cables will really mess up rotor blades, and guess what they can do to turboprops on a fixed wing?" He quickly pulled up and away from the bridge and the ridgeline, and finally he looked at me and said, "Shit, that stupid stunt I was going to do would have killed both of us." "Yup" is all I said.

We continued our get-to-know-the-area flight by buzzing the Green Beret base on the summit of Nui Ba Den before heading for the Cambodian border, where I shared my recent experience with a 37 mm anti-aircraft battery. Our fuel level indicated that we should return to base, and we discussed what we had seen and where we went, with him asking many questions about flying in the weather and dealing with enemy ground fire and identifying fire support bases with airstrips that could handle a Mohawk.

After landing, we walked together for the debriefing, and I took my .38 out of its protective bag and unloaded it as we walked. He looked at my revolver, which was brand new, and showed me his .38, which looked like it had been in the bottom of a well for years. I sincerely doubted that it would even fire if you pulled the trigger. "Where did you get that thing?" I asked. He replied, "This is what they gave me. Can I have yours, since you are so short? What do you have left for time in-country, less than two weeks?" I did have only two weeks or less before I would go home, and usually you did not have to fly unless you wanted the flight time, so I said, "Sure, you can have it; take good care of it because it shoots very well." He handed me his gun and took my .38, and he looked like a kid in a candy shop. We debriefed, but unfortunately I never got to fly with him again because our schedules did not coincide.

I found out when I got back to the States and reported back to Fort Huachuca that my young lieutenant friend and caretaker of my .38 flew into the side of the ridge near the bridge during a nighttime rainstorm. He either forgot that he was supposed to fly parallel to the river and directly over the riverbank or else simply miscalculated and let the wind push him too close to the ridge.

27

Short-Timer
and Finally Home

My time was nearly up for my in-country flying experience. I was within a week of processing out of Vietnam and only flew daytime VR missions when I was told to collect my personal gear (which had been stored since I had arrived in the country) and to turn in my weapon. When I arrived at the depot to retrieve my duffle bag and turn in the lieutenant's .38, the armory sergeant looked at it and said, "This thing has seen much better days," and threw it into a bin that contained other damaged or unusable weapons. I collected my duffle bag and proceeded to the out-processing building and received my orders to depart Vietnam and, more important, my flight home schedule.

I boarded the 707 in Bien Hoa, the same place where I had arrived twelve months earlier, and we took off, headed for Oakland, California. As we left the ground, a full planeload of GIs cheered. I looked out my window and said goodbye to Vietnam.

We must have refueled somewhere, but I don't remember where, and finally touched down on U.S. soil in California. We were bused to the Army depot/processing facility in Oakland, where we were evaluated medically, given a steak dinner and fitted with a new dress green uniform complete with all of our earned medals and ribbons. We were also given airline tickets to the city where we wanted to go and taken to the airport.

I had heard and read about the protests and the treatment that returning troops had received from people who opposed the war, and I, like most of the other Vietnam vets, didn't know what to expect at the airport or on the plane. As I walked through the airport, I noticed several people staring at me, but no one said or did anything. When I arrived at my gate for boarding, I checked in at the counter and then was ignored by the airline employees and other passengers. I didn't realize just how offensive I was to these people, who viewed me as a baby killer and who knows what else they were told to believe about Vietnam vets. When the time came to board the plane, I was given a wide berth until I reached my seat. Only a couple of people acknowledged me as I sat in my seat at the window. I could hear several men and women close to my age sitting a few rows back making comments about me, but they never confronted me, as I had heard happened to many returning vets on their flights home. I was ignored by everyone except the flight attendant who was required to ask me whether I wanted anything. I asked for a Coke and then fell asleep for the long flight back to New England.

The plane landed in Hartford, and I was greeted by my wife and baby daughter, who had been born two weeks after I arrived in Vietnam. I didn't receive the official news of her birth until an additional three weeks had passed, as the Red Cross could not find me in Vietnam to give me the telegram announcing the birth of my daughter and my wife's good health.

I had a month of leave before we had to drive west and report to Fort Huachuca for me to complete my military obligation. The trip across the country was fun except for our first day on the road heading to southern Connecticut to visit some of my wife's relatives. My father-in-law had sold us his 1966 Buick LeSabre, which was a great car to drive cross-country. However, as we got near our destination in Connecticut, I heard noises coming from the rear tire well and, looking in my side mirror, saw black chunks of material coming out of the tire well. I immediately pulled off the road and discovered, to my horror, that the left rear tire was coming apart in chunks and the right rear tire was following suit. The car was not overloaded, as we had only suitcases with clothing in the trunk. For some unknown reason, the tires (which were less than a year old) were self-destructing. The left rear was so bad that I had to replace it with the spare tire.

We didn't have far to go to arrive at an uncle's home but now had a huge problem. I was not going to drive 2,500 miles on tires that could fail at any moment in the middle of nowhere. Luckily, my wife's uncle was employed at a B.F. Goodrich factory nearby and took our car the next day and had new tires installed, including the spare. Another example of human kindness, even if it was from a relative. We found out later that the tires that had failed were part of a batch that had not cured properly during the manufacturing process and they could be replaced by the tire store that sold them.

We had plenty of time to get to Arizona, and we made the most of it by stopping early at motels that had swimming pools, as this was June and the weather was great. We went through Colorado, as we wanted to see the Rocky Mountains; we drove up through the Loveland Pass (there was not a tunnel then) and had fun throwing snowballs while dressed in shorts and short-sleeved shirts. We also drove through Monument Valley and were amazed at the rock formations (we had nothing like this in New England); then it was on to the Grand Canyon and finally to Phoenix, Tucson and Fort Huachuca.

My new first sergeant was able to acquire fantastic on-post housing for us, and we were amazed at the view across the twenty-five-mile valley in front of us to the mountains surrounding the valley. At Huachuca, I injured my arm and had several weeks of physical therapy that resulted in a disability. I also, at Christmas, found myself in the hospital suffering from the worst case of the flu, which nearly killed me. I was so badly dehydrated that I couldn't walk, and when my wife drove me to the hospital on Fort Huachuca, I had to be wheeled from the hospital driveway into the emergency room. I spent two days in the hospital before they released me to recuperate at home. In Vietnam, I had experienced lower back problems that kept me grounded for a day or two on a few occasions. I attributed the back pain to the hours spent sitting on the ejection seat, but that is only speculation.

I completed my military commitment and procured a three-month early out to go back to school. We said goodbye to Fort Huachuca and drove cross-country again, arriving just in time for the fall semester. I got my post office job back, applied for the GI Bill education assistance program, and enrolled in school, where I completed my BA. My advisor while I worked on my BA was an active-duty O-6 (full colonel) with a PhD in geography, which was my major. He was assigned to the U.S. Army Natick Labs in Massachusetts, where he was the CO of the new equipment section. He and his staff were tasked with field testing all new equipment—that is, boots, clothing, hats and gloves, backpacks, prepackaged meals (MREs) and everything a soldier would use in a field environment. He never mentioned anything about testing new weapons; that was the responsibility of a different group. He told me that he traveled extensively around the world, testing new equipment in all imaginable climatic conditions. He did cold-weather testing in Alaska and shared stories of adventures in the woods with wild animals; I think he hoped that the new tent material could stand up to a Kodiak bear. He loved testing equipment in Central America, where he became a coffee bean expert in his spare time. He was close to retirement age, and, due to his testing and evaluation position, he had contacts in several government agencies.

I told my advisor that I was looking for a new job away from the postal service, and since I was ready to graduate, he gave me the names of several people in different government agencies to contact after talking with me and discovering that I was a 1st Cavalry Vietnam vet and had valuable experience in aerial mapping. I followed up with his leads and completed several lengthy job application forms, which led to me interviewing with multiple government agencies that dealt with mapping and surveillance activities. For various reasons, I did not accept the jobs offered to me. One of the agencies (whose name I will not use) was having congressional budget problems at the time, and I assessed that it was not an appropriate time to join. I was promised promotions in the postal service at the same time that I interviewed with the other agencies and decided to stay where I was. Unfortunately, the promotions never happened due to budget cuts, which led me to my new job as a corporate fleet manager at a Fortune 500 company.

While all the above was occurring, I stayed in school and earned my MBA degree and continued my education, with a second master's degree in counseling psychology. During this time our son was born.

The Fortune 500 company I was with was bought by another company, and my fleet manager position disappeared as a result of the acquisition. Before I lost my job, I was hired by a British car manufacturer to be its representative for New England and Boston to Buffalo, calling on the dealerships that sold its cars and SUVs. This car company moved us to Maryland and we settled in the Annapolis area, where we live today.

An interesting thing about working for this company was that I became a certified off-road driving instructor and participated in company-sponsored off-road driving programs for customers in several parts of the country. I'll share two off-road driving stories. The first occurred during a Range Rover customer event at which the new Range Rover customer paid a considerable sum of money to attend the off-road driving event while staying at a five-star resort, enjoying skeet shooting, fly fishing, incredible food and getting muddy with a new Range Rover supplied by the company. On this occasion, we had a six-car convoy driving in a national forest near Pike's Peak. The trails we drove on were nothing but fire tracks and were imposing as hell. At lunchtime we called a halt and dove into the basket lunches prepared for us by the resort. There was everything in those baskets, starting with smoked trout and going upward from there. We did not allow alcohol while driving on these events; the customers had to wait until we returned to the resort to have their wine or cocktail.

Our lead driver and we instructors were gathered at the edge of a heavily forested 800-foot-deep ravine with steep rock walls on both sides when our fearless leader motioned across the ravine to the rocks and vegetation and casually mentioned that "over there, those rocks and bushes and trees make a perfect mountain lion and grizzly bear territory, and what is equally interesting, if we were standing over there looking this way, I would say the same thing!" We quickly broke away from the edge of the ravine and told our customers to load up and get into the cars, as we were moving on, NOW!

The second story involves the same kind of drivers and vehicles, but it took place in the mountains of North Carolina. The resort we used was affiliated with Duke University. As usual, the event took into consideration the interests of our wealthy Range Rover owners, and we headed out into another national forest. At lunchtime we were far away from civilization, and there was a wild river close to the fire road we were using. Just for the fun of it, I started whistling the tune from "Dueling Banjos," and as if on cue, two guys emerged from the woods and stared at us. They couldn't believe their eyes, because parked in a grove in front of them were five shiny new vehicles that couldn't possibly have been driven up the trails and through the woods to that location. Both men had rifles or shotguns (they never came close enough for us to tell), and each man had three or four dead squirrels hanging from a rope attached to his waist. Everyone looked at each other, and finally our lead driver headed toward the men and said, "We are leaving right now so that we don't interfere with your hunting." One of the men simply looked at him and us and nodded. We loaded up faster than we did when we thought that mountain lions were around us and headed quickly down the trail and off the mountain. Everyone in that convoy thought that each of us, clients and instructors, deserved a strong cocktail, and we lost no time in getting back to the resort and the bar.

During this time, my wife started her own educational consulting company representing publishers that produced books for the K–12 school market and public library market. I burned out of the car business, as I was tired of dealing with disgruntled customers and dealerships, and joined my wife in her business. Good move on my part!

It has taken me a long time (50-plus years) to think about that year in Vietnam and put my memories onto paper. I found around fifty photos of Vietnam, most of which I didn't remember I had, and included several of them in this work. I am sure that sometime later I will remember a situation and ask myself, "How could you forget to include that in your stories?" I guess that we can only remember so many things that happened so long ago, even after making pages of notes.

Thank you for reading and sharing my memories!

28

Military Awards and Service History

I received my draft notice in late spring of 1967 and enlisted in the Army that summer, reporting to Fort Dix, New Jersey, for basic training and then going on to advanced training at Fort Huachuca, Arizona, at the Airborne Sensor School. In late May 1968, I received my orders for Vietnam and was assigned to the 1st Calvary Division's aerial surveillance and target acquisition platoon based in Phu Bai, Vietnam, in I Corps. While serving in Vietnam, I was awarded the Army Commendation Medal, National Defense Service Medal, Vietnam Service Medal, and Air Medals with the 1st through 17th Oak Leaf Clusters, and I was expert with both the M-14 rifle and the M-16 rifle. I was promoted to E-5, specialist 5th class, in Vietnam and was on the E-6 promotion list at Fort Huachuca, but I separated from the Army with an early out to return to school before I could be promoted to staff sergeant. I served on active duty until late June 1970, when I received an honorable discharge and a three-month early separation to return to college.

There is a large discrepancy in my number of Air Medals awarded. I discovered that nearly three months of my flight time were not calculated in my Air Medal count. I am missing flight hours for June 1968, July 1968 and most of August 1968. During this time period, I was flying daily both daytime missions and nighttime infrared missions. I calculate conservatively that I am missing 400 hours of flight time, which would equate to an additional 16 Air Medals, bringing my total to 33 Air Medals. I don't know why these hours were not included in my totals, but they weren't.

Index

151